ERIC DELVE

TO
BOLDLY
GO

Discover your destiny, and how you can fulfil it.

D0993530

Published in the UK in 2013 by Echoes In Eternity Publishing

PUBLISHING

WEB: www.ericdelve.com
TWITTER: @EricDelve
FACEBOOK: www.facebook.com/EricDelveUK

ISBN 978-1-909425-41-5
e-ISBN 978-1-909425-42-2

DESIGN:
Art Direction: Dan Hasler
Cover and Graphic Design: Matthew Varah Wilson
Graphic Design: Samuel Bloomfield
www.messagecreative.com

IMAGE CREDITS
The following images used are taken from www.flickr.com and used under the (cc) 2.0 license.

We would like to thank the following:

Chapter 1	FLICKR_ZACH DISCHNER
Chapter 2	FLICKR_NASA GODDARD PHOTO AND VIDEO
Chapter 3	FLICKR_CHARLES ATKEISON
Chapter 4	FLICKR_NASA GODDARD PHOTO AND VIDEO
Chapter 5	FLICKR_X-RAY DELTA ONE
Chapter 6	FLICKR_JIMBOWEN0306
Chapter 7	FLICKR_NASA GODDARD PHOTO AND VIDEO
Chapter 8	FLICKR_JURVETSON
Chapter 9	FLICKR_THE WANDERING ANGEL
Chapter 10	FLICKR_RIELLIE CALDERONIE
Chapter 11	FLICKR_SEIER+SEIER_PAINT
Epilogue	FLICKR_NASA GODDARD PHOTO AND VIDEO

First published in the UK in 2013 by Echoes In Eternity Publishing

CONTENTS

DEDICATION

This version of To Boldly Go is dedicated to my wife Pat, whose courage, loyalty and love never cease. I have learned so much from her.

Also to our children and their spouses: Sarah, Glenn and Cathy, Joanne and Luca, Rebekah and Wayne, Andy and Suzie; Grace and Matty. Not forgetting the grandchildren: Jack, James, Cameron, Leia, Casper, Joseph, Tomaso, Clio, Anouk and "the bump" shortly to arrive! We're so proud of you all.

I am hugely thankful to Barbara Faiers Thompson who took an old book and made it part of the IT age. To Peter Ellis who enables me to communicate in this new era.

To the Rhino Club whose members have become friends closer than brothers: Nick Battle, John Pressdee, Mike Mitton, Russ Parker, Steve Hepden, Paul Bennison, Pat Lynch (member in absentia), and Ian Petit (member in Gloria).

Thank you all for being means of grace.

INTRO

Often, people say in forewords, you won't be able to put this book down. I encourage you to do the opposite. Don't just skim it. Read carefully and thoroughly, a chapter at a time. Work out its implications for your life. If you feel broken and scarred, this book will help restore your spiritual health. It'll be like soothing ointment to your wounds.

Eric Delve holds nothing back in this book. He weaves together his years of world-wide experience as an evangelist, life as a pastor and his journey with Christ into the heart of God. His honesty and realism are breath-taking. He shares himself; his successes, failures, insights and what is really on his heart. Each chapter speaks of the integrity of a man who, through the ups and downs of life, has remained faithful to God because he has glimpsed His Kingdom.

The message comes through time after time: 'Live originally, not as a boring stereotype... use your life wisely... it matters what you do.' It's a call to urgent reassessment of our lives and our churches, in the light of God. He is near and involved, sustaining and upholding his creation. He has revealed Himself in history, the pinnacle of which is Christ. We can know God, and that He has a plan for our lives. This is a wake-up call to Christians, to be aware of the kind of God who saved us, and the implications of the message of Jesus to the world we are in.

Never in my lifetime has it been as important for Christians to face the issues at stake; 'unless we grasp the reality and vital importance of spiritual things we will live in the emptiness of materialism.' Surely nobody can look at the state of the world and be satisfied with things as they are. But this is not only true of the world.

Christians are painfully aware that we're not what we should be – neither are our churches. This book meets us right there.

Eric deals with many thorny issues which people ask me about all over the world. He answers questions about our personal calling and mission, and our struggle against sin. He takes on apathy in the Church and calls us to have huge visions, of a God who constantly surprises us. There's a call to gutsy godliness and practical advice on everyday holiness. We see the vital need for renewed commitment to the Bible and prayer, in the spiritual battle. Before us is the final vision of reaching the heart of God – experiencing the Kingdom of Heaven for eternity. In Christ we can know who we are, and what we're on Earth to do. We only live once, and we're responsible to live this life to the full for God. Yet our hope isn't just for this life. Ahead of us lies the 'crown of glory'.

I commend this book highly. We are people with a glorious destiny, when the only destiny the world is heading for is destruction. The call is going up around this country and the whole world. It is time to seize the day – not for ourselves but for Him who made us. He died for us, rose and now reigns for us. He longs that as His people, we should do the work He set us apart for before the creation of the world. Will we let this moment pass us by?

I pray that reading this book will enable you to 'press on to take hold of that which took hold of you'. For over thirty years Eric has been a friend and inspiration to me. May you find him to be the same for you.

Revd. Canon J.John

A BIT OF HISTORY

In 1954 a young American evangelist called Billy Graham came to England to preach in a huge London venue called Harringay Arena. It was packed out for twelve weeks night after night. The effect was stupendous. London was shaken and the whole nation impacted. Billy Graham almost decided to stay in Britain indefinitely. Musing on that possibility in 1963, David Frost wrote,

> 'What would have happened? Would we have become a nation as dull and narrow-minded as some of his followers? Or a nation as vibrantly alive and flagrantly Christian as Dr Graham himself? Or what? I wish he'd stayed.'

What a terrifying question. The Church still claims to proclaim the good news of Christ, the wisdom and dynamic of God. Yet so many of us live lives that are 'dull', without character, pale and grey. How could the message of the living God in Christ produce people so bland, innocuous and irrelevant, so capable of being ignored, so – boring?

There is only one answer – an absence of Jesus Christ from our Christianity. Our only message is him. And we cannot be God's messengers unless we are living the message.

PROLOGUE... CAPTAIN'S LOG

The emergency session of the Inter-Galactic Council of the Heavens was nearly over. At its secret meeting place 'somewhere in the cosmos' debate had raged for a small eternity.

Finally the Archangel surveyed the assembly. 'We are all agreed then? There is only one man who can deal with this crisis – we must send for him.'

The decision was made. Momentous silence descended. The Archangel reached out; his hand hovered for a moment before coming down on the super-emergency call button.

Instantly the call raced across space and time until its silent clamour reached the ears of the Rev. Rock Firm, quiet-spoken, gentle minister of St Edburga-the-Less Church, Megalopolis. He stiffened for a moment and then rose from the table at which the Ladies' Bright Hour Committee were debating the annual outing to Brightsea.

'Please excuse me, Ladies,' he said. 'Duty calls me – an unexpected need.'

The ladies smiled – they were used to their dear minister and his rather absent-minded ways.

Outside the door of the room he was transformed. Dashing into his private vestry he shut the door. So fast that all movement was a blur, he peeled off his outer garments revealing a purple cape resting on powerful shoulders which were encased in a tight-fitting blue costume. Powerful muscles rippled as his mighty thighs propelled him towards the window. Grabbing his special Super-Amplified Bible he launched himself upward from the window-sill.

A few blocks away some church members emerging from a prayer meeting looked up in amazement.

'Is it a bird?'

'Is it a plane?'

No,' said a quiet voice, 'it's Superchristian.'

Ineffective, mild-mannered Christian sap Elmer J. Crud continued looking long after the purple missile had vanished from view. The others drifted home leaving him standing alone on the church steps. Sadly at last he turned to go, his shoulders drooping in despair, failure in his eyes! 'Oh gosh, Superchristian,' he whispered, 'I wish I could be like you.'

CHAPTER 1
NO FINAL
FRONTIER

I have often watched *Star Trek*. The final phrases stick in my mind

> Space – the final frontier:
> These are the voyages of the Starship Enterprise;
> Its on-going mission:
> To explore strange new worlds;
> To seek out new life-forms and new civilisations;
> To boldly go **where no one has gone before!**

But here's a question – **is it**? Is space truly the final frontier? Physicists facing our universe in the light of discoveries might well query that. And if, as seems increasingly likely, there is a Creator, the **final** frontier will be a huge gateway into the unlimited wonder of the Maker of all things.

THE LONG SEARCH

We began the search the moment we were born – maybe even while in the womb – a quest for identity, meaning, and love. More significant, but unrealised by most of us, is that Love is searching for us. Not the emotional lightning strike of being 'in love', nor the burning of physical desire, but the real thing: passionate, selfless, unending. However there is a 'but'. We can find that kind of intensity unsettling – asking uneasily 'what do you want? We may discover ourselves edging towards the door – if only we could find one. It is one thing to search, but something else to have someone searching for us. It may be easier to pretend there's no one there. If we do that, our need for relationship may ambush or unexpectedly embarrass us. In an interview in the *Daily Telegraph,* August 31st 1992, Richard Dawkins, author of *The Selfish Gene* and *The God Delusion,* explains his reasons for not believing in God to Mick Brown.

The article concludes with this quote:

> ' "I've contemplated a tropical rainforest and felt a tremendous sense of awe, or worship ..."
> There is a pause. He didn't mean to say that.
> "Not, of course, that there is anything **to** worship." '

Fascinating. Apparently confident, the human race come of age needing neither God's company nor his help – yet perhaps subconsciously uneasy.

THE RISEN CHRIST IS THE KEY

Strangely, Dawkins is not so far from the way many Christians live. The prophetic analyst of modern Christianity A. W. Tozer wrote: 'Most Christians of my acquaintance live as pro-tem atheists.' He observed that most of us believe, 'Christ died for us' and 'Christ will come again', yet live in the present as if God were dead. Paul the apostle wrote that if Christ had not been raised, our faith can only give us a bit of spurious comfort in our brief lives and: *'we are of all people most to be pitied'* [1] – an old translation reads *'we are of all men most miserable.'* It may not be strictly accurate but it's still true. Without the deep friendship of the risen Christ, Christianity can only disappoint, and make us miserable.

So how we see Jesus is crucial. If we view him from a purely human understanding, Jesus, the one from heaven becomes like us – just another prisoner of our world. Together in chains, we wearily plod an earthbound path, and nothing raises our heads. But the heart of the Christian is the conviction that Jesus is alive – human yet divine. As human he retains the scars and scale of his life in Roman Palestine. As divine, he is a colossus uniting heaven and earth in himself. Somehow, through him heaven touches us, and every moment of our lives is shot through with heavenly meaning. Through him earth in us is taken up into heavenly places, and begins to be transformed. When our search at last brings us to Jesus, we discover that all along he was searching for us. Then in him we begin the most exciting journey ever – into the heart of God.

SOMETHING MUST HAPPEN

Christianity is not merely a philosophy, a system of belief or a code of ethics. Those things emerge from a life lived to the full in relationship with Jesus. The problem is, adhering to the truths of the resurrection and ascension, we can still live as if Jesus were really dead. We are people in limbo – neither dead, nor truly alive. Not sufficiently heavenly minded to be of any earthly use, not earthly minded enough to be of any heavenly use, we find no real place in the outworking of heavenly strategy. In a spiritual desert where many sicken and die, we may wearily carry on, hiding our desperate emptiness. There are moments when the embers flare into life – only to die down leaving us greater failures than we were before.

We know the Archangel proclaimed, 'With God nothing is impossible'. Yet still we say 'Nothing happened'. And we don't get it – this means we are no longer with God, for 'nothing' is impossible **with** him. 'Something' must happen where he is! Many crises call for urgent attention. But the most desperate need of our world is for us as Church to be identifiably like Jesus, with a presence that can only be explained by him in us.

CHRIST LIVES IN US – THE ONLY HOPE

God made us to be like Him, living works of art reflecting his love, joy, creativity, truth, purity, and wonder. In one word – his GLORY. When Paul the apostle writes about our failure as humans he says, we have 'all… come short of the glory of God'. Only one man ever perfectly lived like that – and it isn't me! Just ask my wife and children. But Jesus did it. The rest of us have failed. So there is hope. Paul puts it like this: 'Christ in you, the hope of GLORY'.

Jesus died and rose again not just so we could be forgiven. He did it all, so that we could be radically changed. God has no rest home for Christians who accept defeat, or resign their commission on the grounds that life in heaven's army is too tough. He expects us to win. So it must be possible, even if we have failed again and again, or gone far away from him.

The good news says to the failure, 'You **can** make it'. Into the far country of despair comes a whisper of hope. God's kingdom is 'at hand': so close you can stretch out your hand and take your Big Brother's hand. There is a way out, a high way, a protected way. So why doesn't it work? Why have millions of Christians tried to be changed, only to be defeated over and over until dull resignation sets in: 'Guess I'll always be a loser'. (Now I'm repeating Satan's lies.)

What's wrong? What's missing is the total absence of any assurance that my life means anything. It feels like whatever happens to me; my small struggles, occasional victories and devastating defeats, are of no real consequence. I've forgotten. Christ has come to live **in me** to give me the hope of glory in this world and in Eternity. God cares so much for me that he has carefully crafted a destiny for me – and everybody else too.

ROBBED OF TRUE VALUE

Like many ministers and evangelists, I have been faced with Christians saying, 'I wish I could be like you'. They might change their minds if they spoke to my family! Such people have no vision of their own destiny. They don't understand 'the son of God loved **me** and gave himself for **me**'. We are too slow to realise that God made me to be me – and not anybody else. He delights in the 'me-ness' of me, no matter how odd I may be. If I don't know that, I might get encouragement by reading stories of others whom God has used. But not if I wind up believing I'm not special – they are.

The best Christian biographies tell us that when an extraordinary God gets hold of an ordinary person, an irresistible combination is the result. Yet too many never experience the real adventure of living with God. This reduces the sense of their own value. So they settle for being 'just an ordinary Christian'. Even worse, they begin to believe in a celebrity value system, where Christian leaders and 'names' are automatically of higher value than others in the church.

I once received a letter from a man who said that he was 'only a lavatory attendant'. The Bible knows nothing of such judgements. The only hierarchy in heaven is the hierarchy of Christlikeness. The real questions won't ever appear in 'Hello' magazine! How well do you know God? How much do you love him? How deeply has his nature changed yours?

YOU ARE THE ONLY ONE

God has no 'special' people. Some he uses in more obvious ways than others but all humans are 'special' to him. He is a father and a mother – not a spiritual industrialist with an endless production line turning out standard modules of spiritual life. His fatherhood and motherhood, like his loving, are infinite in their capacity. You are his child. He knows your name, and your family, and has called you by name into his own Family. God knows you and loves you – personally. I once told someone, 'God loves you'. She responded, 'Well, he loves everybody doesn't He?' True, but it is not that God loves me because he loves everybody. The truth is he loves the whole world because he loves each individual – one at a time – including you.

You are precious, loved, and longed for – the child of a glorious, great, loving Father. It began long before you were born. He loved you even before he ever breathed the galaxies into being. However good or bad your earthly father may have been, however bad a child you may have been, God is your true Dad. He fathered you in eternity before all things.

Why you especially? Because you are unique, a once-only expression of the living God: made to hear, see and know him like no one else ever before. Your purpose then is to unveil before the watching creation, the revelation of God that can only be unveiled through you. You are physically, genetically, intellectually, emotionally, psychologically never to be repeated. God has only this one chance in this universe to reveal the facet of his character that is uniquely for you to know and show. There will never be another one like you!

Maybe your reaction is to say 'Thank God' – you would be right whatever your reason! You are not an accident. Neither Satan's opposition nor man's rebellion has any effect on God's sovereign act of creation. He alone gives to each human that unique expression of his own life that is the soul, the spirit of a person. You and I really do matter.

Each of us is infinitely precious, but only a small part of the whole. When God finally puts us all together in the mystery the Bible calls the body of Christ, then his true incandescent glory will be seen. Here in a fallen world its revelation is intermittent. When the Eternal Day dawns, the brilliance of our Heavenly Father will blaze out of each of us as we interact in the Great Dance of love, joy, creativity and laughter.

WHY SATAN HATES YOU

Satan hates God. Humans are made in God's image. They remind him of God – so he hates **you**. By attacking the body and mind, breaking the heart and wrecking the psychology, he continually tries to ruin God's beautiful masterpiece. He knows that by hurting you, he can cause God pain. He knows how important you are to God.

Why? Because the most fundamental thing about God is – he's a Father. Jesus called him Dad. Throughout Eternity from beginning to end he's the Father of Jesus. One of his names for Jesus is 'The Word'. "This is my Son and he says everything there is to say about me. I'm so proud of him." Jesus is full of God's creativity, intelligence and imagination – so he made you! That makes you also a child of the Creator, a little word from God. He loves you. Like any good father God has dreams for his children. His vision for you is amazing, more exciting than anything you could produce alone. Don't think you can't make it. Jesus promised that if we have even a tiny seed of faith we can hook in to our Destiny "And nothing will be impossible for you". We become People without Limits.

Satan hates that idea! He'll do all he can to cripple you and stop you accessing your Destiny. But your adventure is to find that Destiny and live it. Jesus called this 'the good news of the kingdom of God'. Here on earth, humans can give messed up lives to the living eternal God; so that he comes to live in them and the whole of life begins to be an expression of God. It may be scary – very! Difficult – often. Boring – never! They are living the kingdom of God, and

God's splendour starts to stream out from them.

However many universes there are in God's multi-dimensioned creation, all of them are waiting – for you to be revealed as truly a son or daughter of God. So rejoice. Be glad where you are at this moment. Thank God he made you. It was a once-only creative act designed to unfold his nature in this world, and in the eternal reality of "the heavenlies".

They are the natural dwelling of the eternal God, his archangels, angels, heavenly princes and powers. This same God has fathered you through Christ so that all these beings may know more of him. It may seem crazy, but the angels of God can never know him fully, unless you become what you are finally meant to be: happy, holy and loving, an ordinary person filled with an extraordinary God – an irresistible combination. Like light passing through a prism, the pure outshining of the Heavenly Father will pass through us to reveal all the complex beauty of his heart.

WHY SATAN FEARS YOU

But others inhabit his heavenly realm – Satan, king of emptiness, and all his deceiving spirits, hate-filled fallen angels, demonic hordes. He reigns over the world's darkness, torment, abuse and despair. He demands God's throne and claims this world for his own. Yet God has destined him for destruction. And the final blow to his ambitions will come from the inhabitants of this planet. The whole rotten, tottering edifice of Satan's kingdom will be brought crashing down by the church militant here on earth. Jesus gave him a mortal wound at Calvary. That will be exploited by the Christians who proclaim it, and so accomplish his final defeat.

> 'So the huge dragon, the serpent of ancient times, who is called the Devil and Satan, the deceiver of the whole world, was hurled down upon the earth and his angels were hurled down with him. Then I heard a great voice in heaven cry: "Now the salvation and the power and the kingdom of our God and the authority of his Christ has come! For the accuser of our brethren has been thrown down from this place, where he stood before our God accusing them day and night. Now they have conquered through the blood of the Lamb and through the word to which they bore witness. They did not cherish life even in the face of death!"'[3]

What an amazing passage. Hard to believe but it is the sober truth. We are to accomplish this victory. You have a part to play. We are told Jesus will destroy the enemy by the brightness of his appearing and the breath of his mouth. That brightness shines from you, and his breath rests on you. You are a greater person than you knew!

LOVE IS OUR SECURITY

Jesus turned to the disciples and said, 'The Father loves you'. Enormous! The great Father-Creator is responsible for a universe which stretches out in all directions from this earth for at least 20,000 million light years. He is instantly, fully, always present in every part of it. Moving so fast that he is always everywhere, therefore always at rest, he is the living God. This unimaginable greatness is summed up for us by Jesus as 'the Father'. But he was more definite, 'the Father **himself**'. In other words the very core of his being, the essence, the centre, the heart of God loves **you**. Contemplate it with wonder. Meditate on it and rejoice. 'The Father himself loves you.'

How should we respond?

David's response in Psalm 18 was passionate;

> *'I love thee, O Lord, my strength. The Lord is my rock, and my fortress, and my deliverer, my God, my rock, in whom I take refuge, my shield, and the horn of my salvation, my stronghold.'*

Fierce love and driving certainty live in those lines. David was a man of action who had proved the total worth and dependability of the God of action. The intimacy of his relationship is shown by the word 'thee'. When I was a child they told me this was the language of respect and of proper distance – the right servile tone for a poor human to use to the eternal God. That was mistaken. This is the language of closeness, of love. 'How do I love thee, let me count the ways' wrote Robert Browning to Elizabeth Barrett. Today we don't often use 'thee' and 'thou' in our praying, because it doesn't really fit modern speech. But it is worth remembering that the 'you' we talk to is close to us – closer than father, lover, friend – and different from the same 'you' known to our fellow Christians. But we are not all Davids.

YOUR CHOICE MATTERS

Micah's world was like our own. Wealth, corruption and injustice marched with oppression of the poor; while orthodox religion provided a false cover for people who did not know God. So Micah appealed to individuals to stand out against the tide, stand up for their God – and above all, to know him.

> *'What is good has been explained to you, man; this is what the Lord asks of you: only this, to act justly, to love tenderly, and to walk humbly with your God.'*[3]

Your God – not someone else's God, but yours. No question in Micah's mind as to the God they were to know. The personal God of holiness, truth and gladness, the eternal God of Abraham, Isaac and Jacob. Precisely because he was the God of those men: the same God – but not the same to them; he was the God each man of Israel was to seek and know. Any parent worth their salt knows that each child is fascinatingly different from the other, and is therefore a slightly different parent to each one. Thank God! This is the way he is. He wants to lead us into a real relationship, a love affair with the everlasting one, not just for our sake but also for his delight.[4]

YOU MATTER

You really do matter. The way you live makes a small but real difference to the out-working of the plans of almighty God. Put that way it sounds crazy – but it is the truth. Evangelists (and I am one) are always saying 'God has a purpose for your life'. We need to apologise, because we have said it so often it has become a truism; a saying so common as to sound boring. But the opposite is true. This is the pulsating heart of the message of Jesus Christ. 'You can be what you are meant to be, by God's power, as you yield to him as King.' Draw back and God's unfolding purpose for all things will be hindered or thwarted for a while. If you give him the government of your life, the kingdom of God will move onward in you, and you will become a beachhead of truth, peace, joy and love in a sordid world. There are no limits to what God may accomplish through you. Satan wants to put a barrier before you to stop you. But you are a child of the eternal Father – moving in his destiny. For you there is no final frontier!

How to start? You can begin by believing and by committing that faith to the Father in a prayer, like this maybe:

'Father, my Father,
I thank you that you love me
and have always loved me.
Thank you that you know why you made me.
Thank you that I mean something in your plan.
In weakness with all my failures,
my good points and bad points
I give myself to you.
By your power freely given,
I will be what I am meant to be.
Let your will be done in me.
I trust you.
Amen.'

Does it work? Can God take ordinary failures and make them heavenly success stories? What we want to do now is to look at some of the evidence.

CHAPTER 2
MISSION ACCOMPLISHED

'I have fought the good fight, I have finished the race, I have kept the faith. From now on there is reserved for me the crown of righteousness, which the Lord, the righteous judge, will give me on that day.'[1]

Captain Christopher Pike to a drunken James Tiberius Kirk just battered in a bar brawl: "So your dad dies and you can settle for a less than ordinary life. But you feel like you were meant for something better – something special. Enlist in Star Fleet… Your father was Captain of a Starship for twelve minutes. He saved eight hundred lives – including your Mother's – and yours. I dare you to do better." (Star Trek 2009)

JESUS – THE TRUE HUMAN

"**T**he men in the church are so wet! Where are the real men?" The speaker was female, young and indignant. I had just spoken at the Youth Fellowship and was staying with her parents. I had exulted in the manhood of Jesus and his power as a leader of men, so she was entitled to ask the question. Later she moved to New Zealand where she found and married a real man – a Maori Christian! What has happened to our concept of manhood in the church? John Eldredge makes an interesting comment on the unhealthy power of Church culture in his seminal book, 'Wild at Heart'. "God made men to be dangerous – the church has trained them to be nice!" Take Charles Wesley's children's hymn, 'Gentle Jesus, meek and mild'. Language and culture change. That famous first line means something quite different today – possibly 'Gentle Jesus, weak and ineffective'.

Such a concept dominates much church thinking. Thousands of children emerged from Bible class with the impression that Jesus was impossibly nice, rather effeminate, totally unrealistic about the world, and unable to cope with its problems. They grow into adults who see him as the proverbial Innocent – unwilling to face the shadow side of humanity. Insulated from the world's nastiness by his own niceness, he finally succumbed to the bad men because he was too weak to do anything else. Too often this caricature resides in the hearts of Christian men. They feel forced to choose between spirituality built on this fake vision of Jesus, and a macho manliness in which hatred and aggression are principal ingredients. What makes a real man, or a real woman? One word – courage. Britain's wartime leader Winston Churchill said, "Courage is rightly esteemed the first of human qualities... because it is the quality which guarantees all others".

What is courage? It is a moral attribute demonstrated in decision-making in daily life, having three vital elements: Face and recognise the thing we really don't want to think about. Recognise in it the root of fear and reject its control. Do what we know to be right, whatever the consequences may be. Jesus was a real man, the best, bravest and toughest there ever was. And in all he endured he was sustained by his destiny. Many of us know that his life fulfilled hundreds of prophecies. With the benefit of hindsight, it can all look cosily inevitable – God's programme running on schedule. But the gospels give us another picture: Jesus was subject to temptations, assailed by sudden doubts and weariness. Yet he kept going, sustained by the Father's love. In the reality of that relationship he held on to God's purpose.

THE CHILD IS FATHER TO THE MAN

His conviction was real by the time Jesus was twelve. That year's visit to the Temple and participation in Passover celebrations marked his coming of age. Was the trip from Nazareth to Jerusalem the time chosen by Joseph and Mary to tell their son the amazing story of his conception? He saw the gleaming dome of the Temple, the great court of the Gentiles, and Solomon's porch. What did he think, knowing that the first time he had been there as a baby, a holy old man now long dead, had held him and thanked God,

> *'Now at last I can die in peace; for my eyes have seen God's salvation...'*[2]

Although they lived for a time as refugees in Egypt, Jesus and his parents returned to Judea to live a quiet, normal life. His parents seem to have almost forgotten who he really was. The sudden realisation that he had not left Jerusalem with the party heading back to Nazareth, made a mockery of the after-feast carnival atmosphere. They rushed back to the city in panic. Finally they found him, a country boy from despised Nazareth in uncouth Galilee, debating in cultured surroundings with university professors. Luke tells us Jesus was asking them questions. It was the way great scholars taught their pupils. Jesus was engaged in a debate as if with equals! Dr Adam Bradford says from that moment the responsibility for Jesus' training would have passed to the most brilliant scholars of the Temple. Jesus would have been a treasure to be watched over and stewarded. It was their duty to the God of Israel. Only Temple involvement in his education explains how at the age of thirty he became a doctor of the law.[3] But at that moment none of that registered with his parents. Their own guilt feelings showed clearly; 'Son, why have you treated us like this? How could you? Your father and I have been so worried looking everywhere for you.' His reply shows only a genuine puzzlement:

> 'Why did you have to look for me? Didn't you know that I have to be in my Father's house?'[4]

Then he left with them to become a good carpenter, and to await his Father's time. He was obedient to them – his humility born out of his assurance of who he was. There was no need to assert himself, no need to rebel in order to find his identity. He had it and began to grow in it. He increased in respect with God and men. He must have been a good carpenter! And a great student.

THE MAN IS ALWAYS HIS FATHER'S SON

Eighteen years go by and Jesus, now a doctor of the law, goes to see his cousin John. He persuades a reluctant Baptist to dip him in the Jordan River as a sign of repentance for sin – when John knows and Jesus admits he has no sin of which to repent. 'It should be done, for we must carry out all that God requires', he says. Immediately the heavens open. He sees the Spirit of God descending like a dove and settling on him. He hears the voice of God's affirmation, 'This is my son whom I love, I am well pleased with him.' At this moment he consciously joins battle with Satan. The Spirit drives him out into the wilderness to confront the enemy. Nearly six weeks go by. The tempter hits him with every temptation known to the human race. But Satan is beaten: beaten by God's man sustained by the Holy Spirit – with an absolute assurance that he is God's son. At this moment of victory Satan tempts Jesus to misuse his sonship to feed himself; then to deny it by accepting Satan's authority; and lastly to presume on it by acting on a faith not founded in his Father's guidance.

Two of those temptations actually begin with, '**If** you are the Son of God…' He knows if he can destroy Jesus' trust in God as Father, he will make him as weak as any other human. But even here, the relationships in our Trinity God, Father/Son/Holy Spirit, remain firm. Our insecurities so often provide Satan with opportunities for temptation. The chosen battleground between heaven and hell is human nature. It is in his own humanity that Jesus defeats Satan. That is our hope.

THE AUTHORITY OF THE SON AND HEIR

He returns to Galilee ablaze with power and authority. At the synagogue in his home town of Nazareth he reads these words from Isaiah:

> *'The Spirit of the Lord is upon me because he has anointed me to preach good news to the poor. He has sent me to proclaim freedom for the prisoners and recovery of sight for the blind, to release the oppressed, to proclaim the year of the Lord's favour.'*[5]

Closing the book Jesus calmly declares that all these marvellous promises apply to him. In short, he is the Messiah. Strangely stopping in mid-sentence he omits, 'and the day of vengeance of our God'. That awaits him at the cross. He challenges them to repent of Israel's long history of unbelief. In rage they jump up, grab him and lead him to a nearby cliff-top to push him over. But 'passing through the middle of them he went away'! Disappointing, isn't it? A few thunderbolts at least, you might think. But Jesus knew who he was and where he was to die, and he had a lot to do before that. So he quietly slipped away. He alone was not screwed up with fear or tension. So it was simple to calmly walk away. Jesus' assurance of his destiny is something stamped all over the gospels:

> 'I must proclaim the good news of the kingdom of God to the other cities also; for I was sent for this purpose.'[6]

> 'I do nothing on my own but I speak these things as the Father instructed me. And the one who sent me is with me; he has not left me alone, for I always do what is pleasing to him.'[7]

> 'Very truly I tell you, the Son can do nothing on his own, but only what he sees the Father doing.'[8]

These are not the sayings of a person who lived under a heavy burden of rules and regulations, but of someone who moved constantly in a close relationship with his Father. Always sustained by the Holy Spirit, Jesus delighted to obey him moment by moment. He knew his heavenly Dad loved him.

So in spite of the constant strain of the spiritual warfare he was happy. As the psalmist says in Psalm 45 – happiness was poured upon him more than upon any other human being. Put simply, Jesus was the happiest man who ever lived.

THE COURAGE OF THE SON

He knew the world was held captive by the enemy he called 'the prince of this world'. And when he gave him that title he reminded Satan of the limitation of his power. Plus he knew he had come to rescue us by being the ransom paid to the cosmic kidnapper.[9]

> 'And what am I going to say? "Father get me out of this?" No, this is why I came in the first place.'[10]

At the Last Supper the knowledge of his coming death filled Jesus with limitless love for his disciples. In spite of their bitter quarrels and proud refusal to serve each other, he stripped, wrapped a towel around himself, and he washed their filthy feet. This humility was rooted in his certainty that God had given the whole universe into his hands, and the Kingdom of Heaven into the hands of the disciples.[11]

In the garden over the Kidron valley the air was heavy and still. Jesus prayed and the disciples struggled to stay awake. Facing hell, he sweated drops of blood. Suddenly, silence was destroyed by the clash of armour, and darkness torn by military torches. John says Jesus walked forward to meet them *'knowing all that was going to happen'*.[12] The purpose held him –

the one who had set his face to go to Jerusalem – because that was the only place for a prophet to die. Jesus had promised his Father with body, mind and spirit, *'Not my will, but your will be done'*. What a man! The courage it gave was enough. *'Jesus seeing that everything had been completed... said "I'm thirsty".'[13]* He knew what was happening, and that carried him through to triumph: the triumph of the great cry, *'It's done... complete!'[13]* Victory was his.

Jesus' sense of destiny is so obvious. His whole life was consciously the outworking of God's purpose – and for most of that life he was a carpenter, and part-time student. Jesus was a working man and that was his destiny – to live out God's sonship as a manual worker.

WE ARE HIS BROTHERS AND SISTERS

It's also the destiny of the church – to live out God's purpose so that simply in being who we are, we praise him. Thank God, the vast majority of Christians are not preachers, ministers, and evangelists. Those who are must live their faith. Your function in the church is a minor matter, your calling is to be the person, the child of God, that the Father intended from the beginning.

If even the eternal son of God needed a real sense of God's purpose, we obviously need it much more. Jesus was the new Adam – the new model for human beings. His own destiny was clearly stated in Old Testament prophecy because of his special function, as the beginner of a new kind of creation.

We share his nature. Jesus unashamedly calls us his brothers. We should live as he lived – we must believe that God has a purpose and meaning for each of us. Just because it is not written in the Bible, it is no less real than Christ's. This purpose is written in God's heart, and Jesus carries it. As he spreads his strong hands before heaven, all the heavenly beings in time and eternity know that God has intended something for us, and they watch eagerly to see – will it happen?

THE PLODDER WHO WON

It has already happened for some people…

'Second-hand Shoes and Boots' the sign over the door read. Inside the workman's cottage a cheerful little man with a bald head was leading a Bible study in between boot-mending. He was twenty-eight years old, and by no means exciting or dynamic. In fact, he could not have been further from the Hollywood image of a 'hero'. He said of himself, 'I can plod. I can persevere in any definite pursuit. To this I owe everything.' Yet on 31 May 1792, this man preached a sermon which changed the history of the world. Its theme was the need for a missionary society, and was summed up:

> Expect great things from God.
> Attempt great things for God.

The people who heard it were going home after the service when he grabbed the arm of another minister and asked in desperation, 'And are you after all, again going to do nothing?'

Four months later the Baptist Missionary Society was formed – the beginning of the modern Protestant missionary movement. William Carey, the man responsible, said, 'Few people know what may be done till they try and persevere in what they undertake.' At the end of his life he said, 'If God used me no one need despair'.

THE PERSECUTOR WHO WEPT

That sounds very much like something written hundreds of years before by another bald-headed little man, who was also bandy legged! Very different: ambitious, cruel, greedy for money and power – the name Saul of Tarsus rang terror in the ears of the early church, like Himmler to the Jews of Europe in the 1930s. Jesus met this vicious little man and transformed him. He wept over the sins of others and felt deep pain when converts fell away from Christ. As Paul the apostle he said, 'I was the worst of sinners because I persecuted the body of Christ, but God had mercy on me so that in the future even the worst sinners will realise God can save and use anybody!' What held this man to his course? 'God set me apart from birth.' He knew that entering the kingdom of God's son, he had entered upon God's purpose for his life.

THE SKINNY MISSIONARY

The Victorians were given to making heroes, but few of them realised how similar the famous apostle was to a skinny little Yorkshireman called James Hudson Taylor. Deeply sensitive, intense, and given to bouts of deep melancholy, with his frail body he was hardly a big-screen hero. But he knew God wanted China to hear the gospel. Barnsley may not sound the most likely starting point for a world-shattering strategy, but that tough town never had a greater son. 'God give me China,' he prayed, and God heard him. 'I sometimes think that God must have been looking for someone small enough and weak enough for him to use, so that all the glory might be his, and that he found me.' Earlier in his life, this man who revolutionised missionary work said 'a deep consciousness that I was no longer my own took possession of me.' He knew he was special, chosen.

THE BIG FISHERMAN

It took a while before big-hearted, generous, quick-tempered Simon Bar Jonah understood the same thing. Big and outwardly confident, he was deeply flawed by insecurity and guilt, and felt no confidence that he could serve God. He was called three times before he finally capitulated to the call of Jesus on the dockside of Galilee. How often people say like him, 'Go away Lord, I'm not good enough'. The reply comes as it did then, 'Enter God's kingdom and you come under my authority, not yours. I've chosen you to bear fruit. You'll be catching men for God, not fish for dinner.'

This is just a fraction. These men found that Jesus released them into a special pathway that fitted their feet only. Each received a special but not unusual call. Something that made each person that answered it feel gloriously privileged.

God preserved their stories, because he wants us to know this is the way he deals with all human beings – including us. Totally down to earth and practical, such people have an assurance that their lives have heavenly meaning. Other people see their refusal to bow the knee to worldly values, satanic pressure or fleshly indulgence, and know they have been with Jesus. Nobody ever accused such people of not being real men or women!

THE MUDDY MYSTIC

What about the women, God's radiant women? St Teresa of Avila was moving a baggage train from one convent to another. Crossing a flooded river the cart encountered a pot-hole. It crashed into the water. Pulling herself to the bank through the muddy water while her possessions were carried downstream she was heard to say, 'Lord I do not wonder that you have so few friends, when you treat the ones you have so badly'. Yet she endured this and much opposition to keep the flame of faith alive in a decadent church.

JOY UNDER THE JACKBOOT

Corrie Ten Boom endured the hell of Ravensbruck concentration camp sustained by the purpose,

> 'I must tell the world that there is no pit so deep that he is not deeper still'.

Listening night after night as American and British bombers pounded her beloved Germany, Basilea Schlink prayed that Germany would lose the war! She knew God would judge the regime that persecuted Jews and strangers, and felt its guilt so deeply she could pray for defeat!

MOTHERS IN THE KINGDOM

(i) Mother of a People:

Amy Carmichael was beautiful, well-to-do, single, and known as 'Madcap' because of her high spirits and sense of humour. From Northern Ireland, she went as a missionary to India. She rescued hundreds of girls and boys from service as prostitutes in Hindu temples. The Tamils called her Amma, 'mother'. She wrote,

> 'Let me not sink to be a clod
> Make me thy fuel, flame of God'.

Her poems and writings inspired hundreds of men and women to become missionaries too. General Booth was speaking for Jesus when he said, 'Some of my best men are women!'

(ii) Mother of a world-shaker:

One remarkable woman gave the world a truly historic man. Yet for a terrible moment it looked as though he would never live to be six. Susannah Wesley suffered agonies the night the rectory in which she lived caught fire. They thought all eight children were out. But as fire raged through the timber building, the face of little five-year-old John appeared at an upstairs window. Two men made a human ladder and dragged him out seconds before the roof caved in! More and more, John Wesley realised he had been delivered for a purpose. He always said he was 'a brand plucked from the burning'. This driving sense of divine purpose never left him. Sustained by it he made the world his parish.

(iii) Mother of the Despised:

Driven by a sense of God's calling, Jackie Pullinger left London by ship promising God she would disembark wherever he told her. She got off in Hong Kong, set up home in the most dangerous place in the world – the Old Walled City, and started to love people. She learnt Chinese, led junkies to Jesus; and as she taught them how to speak in tongues, she saw them released from their addiction. They became the building blocks of an amazing church. Today she is invited to speak to huge audiences of many thousands – but would still rather talk to one person about Jesus.

THE UNKNOWN CELEBRITIES

These are names we know. But have you ever wondered why God left us those long genealogies, or why large parts of the Old Testament are occupied by lists of names? God knows these names mean nothing to us. Even the most saintly Christian or Jew would struggle to get much inspiration from them. Mostly these names have no known story. That's the whole point. We don't know their stories. God does. To him the names and stories are known, loved and honoured. These anonymous lists proclaim, 'God knows, God cares, all are special to him.'

Jesus said, 'A good shepherd calls his sheep by name'. Each of us is called by name, for some purpose which is ours and ours only. When we turn to Christ, we step out of death into life: out of chaos into creativity, out of nowhere into somewhere. Love makes a nobody into somebody. We become special.

I remember a beautiful young Chinese girl the night she finally committed everything to Jesus Christ in a university mission meeting. She beamed, she was radiant. 'I feel special, I feel special and I feel proud.' Exactly. This was not the vicious puffed-up pride which is hell's imitation. This was the real thing. Pride in belonging to the eternal family of God; the sheer exulting privilege of being a member of Christ.

THE FAT HERO

What about our response to this? Perhaps D. L. Moody can help. A successful Chicago businessman and rising preacher, he was dissatisfied with his life. He knew God had a purpose for him but he could not, would not, let God take charge. In Dublin for a Christian conference, he attended an all-night prayer meeting. The next morning Varley, who had prayed with him through the night, said, 'Moody, the world has yet to see what God will do with a man fully consecrated to him'. Moody pondered and analysed the words for weeks.

'"The world has yet to see what God can do with and for and through a man who is fully and wholly consecrated to him"... a man. Varley meant any man. Varley did not say he had to be educated or brilliant or anything else. Just a man. Well, by the Holy Spirit in me, I'll be that man.'

He weighed 300 pounds, had a face half covered by a bushy beard, spoke in a high-pitched nasal twang, and to the end of his life could not spell. But Dwight L Moody became the greatest evangelist the world had ever seen. Whoever you are, I give you his words to make your own.

Of course, some of God's people faced with His destiny have failed. Does it really matter? It is to the stories of some of them that we turn next. Before we do you may like to meditate on this prayer.

'Oh God,
I look at the apostles and the faith-heroes.
I see that you ask, not for our perfection
but our availability to work in us your miracles.
I offer to you all my gifts, talents, and mistakes,
all the resources of my personality.
Take them and fulfil your purpose for my life
Through Jesus who finished his task.
Amen.'

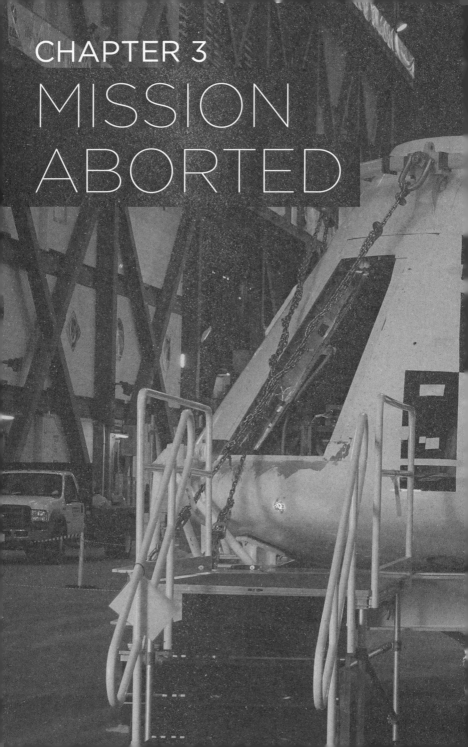

CHAPTER 3
MISSION ABORTED

'To every man somewhere in his lifetime, there comes a special moment, when he is figuratively tapped on the shoulder and offered a chance to do a very special thing, unique to him and fitted to his talents. What if that moment finds him unprepared, unqualified for the work which could be his finest hour?'

(Attributed to Sir Winston Churchill)

THE RIVALS

The baby was hairy. Really hairy! Covered by red hair like a cloak. He had just beaten his twin brother into the world, in fact that one, the smooth one, came in hanging on to 'hairy's' heel.

As she looked at them Rebekah sighed. Such competition even in the act of birth did not bode well. The pregnancy had been difficult, as if a wrestling bout were going on inside her. Finally the pain and discomfort had all become too much. Later it was like a dream, but then it was frighteningly real. Weeping, weary, in deep unending darkness, she wanted to die. But God explained: The babies in her womb would father two rival nations. Eventually the younger child's nation would prevail, and the nation of the older twin would serve them.

THE HAIRY HUNK...

The contrast in physical appearance was matched by a complete contrast of temperament. The firstborn was called Esau – in their language it sounded like 'hairy'. What else could they call him? He grew fast. From the beginning he was hard, tough and fast; a natural athlete. His fast mood changes, sense of humour and impatience for anything that could not be settled quickly, made him clearly a leader of men. The easy confidence that comes with early physical prowess was always his. No matter how fast the wild deer, Esau usually managed to kill one. Isaac, his father, was well pleased. Such a son would make a worthy leader. Of course, Esau seemed to have no real sense of God, but he was young. There was time to learn all that

Isaac had been forty before he married, and sixty when the boys were born. Though he knew his father's God was real, he had never known God in the same way. It had not seemed necessary. Abraham had lived on into Isaac's own old age. His fierce faith in God burned – bright enough for the whole family to the end of his long life. The boys were fifteen when he died and well-schooled in the history of the Covenant. Abraham had entered a holy Agreement and Promise that his family would serve the living God only. This Maker God, grieving over humanity's pain, cruelty and wickedness, had promised Abraham that through his family the whole world would be blessed. Esau had listened dutifully, but his spirit chafed, longing to be out hunting. Then again, the restrictions felt unreasonable. Why not marry outside the family of the covenant? If a person was in love, surely that was enough.

...AND THE FAST-TALKING SMOOTHIE

They named the other boy, Jacob, (the grabber). He listened greedily. Let Esau have his juvenile pursuits – he didn't know what mattered. Jacob did. The most precious thing the family possessed was the Agreement with Promise, the Covenant, and he wanted it. After all, he was Esau's twin, and could easily have been first born. The first-born's birthright was a double share of the property, and stewardship of the Covenant. He didn't really care about the property – he wanted the covenant. How? Daily he brooded on it as he stayed at home helping with the cooking. Smooth Jacob, the hairless wonder. Strangely, the cooking gave him the key – a good thick savoury stew full of vegetables, lentils, and red spices. The fire had brought it to perfection. It simmered gently, little bubbles breaking on the surface and releasing appetising fragrances.

That day had been a bad one for the hunters. Unusually, even Esau had failed to find a deer. No venison roasting over the fire this evening. Disappointment nagged. An empty stomach is hard for an impatient person to bear. As they returned to the camp, the mouth-watering aroma of Jacob's cooking drew Esau as surely the smell of the pitcher plant draws flies. He looked at his brother, they didn't always see eye to eye but surely… a bowl of stew.

'That looks good, really tasty.'

'It is.' Jacob quiet, always watchful, said no more than was necessary.

'I'm starving. Give me some.' Typical Esau, a day out hunting and he was starving.

'Sell you some if you like – for your rights as the first-born.'

Jacob tried to sound casual but there was an edge, a hardness in his voice. Esau eyed him. He had always known that Jacob wanted his position. And he had always resented the responsibility. Slightly angry, he agreed.

'All right. I'm starving to death. What good will my rights do me if I die?'

'Swear it before God – the first-born rights are mine.' And Esau swore a vow giving his rights to Jacob.

THE TERRIBLE CHOICE

He could have changed his mind. He didn't. Seasons passed and the young men matured. At forty Esau decided to marry. He chose two Hittite women – forbidden by the terms of God's Covenant. It was the seal on the bargain made years before with Jacob. That had been the act of an immature and fiery young man. 'What my appetite demands now matters more than some future promise of God.' Choosing these women now just because he wanted to, demonstrated his attitude remained the same. God accepted the bargain.

Isaac, now blind, thought he was dying. Jacob took advantage of his blindness to cheat Esau out of the vital deathbed blessing – passing the blessing of God from the head of the family to the next head of family. At last Esau realised. The line of God's Messiah was his destiny but he had thrown it away, for a bowl of stew, and two pagan women. As he realised what he had lost, the tough hunter broke down and wept. He begged to be able to change the past. But his decision was made. God's destiny now rested firmly on Jacob. But he had still to learn God is not manipulated by our scheming. He does respond to the deepest desires of our hearts.

Eventually Esau forgave Jacob. But his anguish echoed down the years. He could never forget he had thrown away God's purpose. He hadn't lost contact with God. Indeed Jacob later said his face was like the face of God. But the purpose passed to Jacob's family. Over thirteen hundred years later God said through the prophet Malachi, 'Jacob (the nation) I loved and Esau (the nation) I hated.' For after Esau died his nation became implacable enemies of Israel and of God's plans.

THE ETERNAL SEEMS UNREAL

The eternal purpose of God was unreal to Esau compared to what he could see, touch, feel, taste and hear. Indulging his appetites was more important than heavenly reality. Without a sense of destiny, he was powerless to resist temptation. Many of us today are in his position. We believe the right things but live as materialists.

And selfish exploitation of things leads us to see people as our property, also things to be used. In a throwaway society relationships become increasingly disposable.

Rich self-indulgent societies always become sexually immoral societies. The pleasures of sin are pleasurable – for a while. But the fun doesn't last long. Sexually transmitted diseases, the hurt we cause, the guilt and pain we feel, all combine to rob our pleasures of any real sense of joy. Loneliness, disillusion and emptiness, have a nasty habit of reaching back to steal from us even the good times in the past.

We mustn't treat ourselves as if we are just lumps of meat. We are humans made in God's image. We must not fall for the lie of the Devil. God has promised to crown us with his kingdom and eternal glory. That is our destiny: and repentance is the way in.

THERE IS A WAY BACK

A horse exercise ring on Epsom Downs may seem a strange place to find someone praying at three o'clock in the morning – especially a person deliberately kneeling in horse dung. I looked for that place because it fitted my spiritually filthy state. I remembered my Christian home, my calling to Christian service and my rebellion against God's reign. Sliding, then running from God out of control and totally dominated by my false god, my sex drive. I still held tattered shreds of a religious faith around me. They were blown away by a deliberate act of sexual rebellion. I understood my defilement. Tears came.

'Lord, have mercy, I am a sinner. I do repent.'

'My son, what do you want?'

'To be clean. To live in purity.'

'Do you really? If you want the life of fleshly indulgence, that is your choice.'

'I want you. I want your will.'

But it was just a little too routine. Were my tears genuine? Even I couldn't tell.

Suddenly, almost in an audible voice I heard 'Esau sold his birthright for a pot of stew, and afterwards could find no place to repent though he sought it with tears'.

I was being told, 'This is your last chance. Once more like tonight and you will have made Esau's choice. You can be an Esau if you want.' The last thought hung in the air.

In that moment I knew, a person who possesses everything but God has nothing. Christianity is not merely: 'Jesus died for you'; but the reign of God advancing ever deeper into us.

I responded to the voice: 'Lord, I turn from my sin. I will never walk that way again. From now on, you are my King – I will obey you.' Now I can tell people, 'Jesus gives victory over sin.' I have proved it, not without temptation, stumbling, falling and tears; but God has liberated me, and has set me on the road to holiness. Not that I've arrived! But on the evidence, I trust him to get me there.

TWO ROADS LIE WITHIN US

'God has planted eternity in the human heart.'[1]

God inhabits eternity. In planting eternity inside the hearts and minds of people He has made clear our destiny. Each of us is to be a dwelling place for the eternal God – a location in creation where he can be at home. The space in us is God-shaped and God-sized.

Nothing but union with Him will ever fill the void. When I don't let Him into the emptiness, other things rush in to fill it. Evil is the result. But when I let Him take his right place I find the ache dies, peace comes and I am liberated. The roads to hell and heaven lie within us.

I can try to fill the gap with achievements, qualifications and awards, or the adulation and appreciation that flow from people I serve in ministry. All too quickly I start to minister for that purpose. And I'm on a weary treadmill. Only God's "Well done, son" satisfies the longing for affirmation, approval and affection. Only He, the everlasting Father can give me rest.

Our God is so good! He rescues us even from our own stupidity when we call upon him. The tragedy of the son of Manoah clearly demonstrates that.

THE MIGHTY MAN WHO FAILED

God's people had entered the promised land. But they lost his protection by rebelling against Him. The Philistines ravaged the countryside taking anything of value or beauty. God's name was dragged through the dust of Israel's despair.

Then the Lord sent an angel to Manoah's childless wife. Manoah was spiritually sleepy, while his wife was awake to God and obedient to his voice. The messenger was special, 'the angel of the Lord'. Many believe him to have been the son of God before his coming as Jesus Christ. The angel appeared twice, telling her she would have a son who would belong to God. Manoah didn't believe the messenger was from God, and tried him. The angel jumped into an altar fire and ascended in the flame. Manoah finally got it! It was God. When the boy was born they named him Samson. But a strong man needs a strong and godly father to grow up holy. Manoah did not know God well enough.

Samson grew. God's spirit stirred him. He destroyed Philistine crops, slew a lion with his bare hands, decimated whole armies sent against him, and once lifted the Gaza city gates with their posts and lintel on to his shoulders and set them up on the top of a hill. He was incredible. For twenty years the Israelis sheltered behind their hero. However, his upbringing had been dangerously deficient. He didn't get it. His strength was given for God's purpose, not his self-indulgence. His uncut hair was the sign he belonged to God. Eventually this secret was prised from Him by Delilah. But his undisciplined sex life betrayed him, long before Delilah did. She cut off his hair. The Philistines came for him. He thought he still had his supernatural strength. *'He did not know that the Lord had left him.'*

GOD CAN TRANSFORM OUR FAILURE

The Philistines, gouged out his eyes and chained him at the mill-wheel in the prison. Poor stupid Samson, caught by a woman he loved, ridiculed by people who for so long had lived in fear of him. He had betrayed God. God seemed to have abandoned him. But – God was at work. Samson's hair began to grow again. Even when we fail, God's love goes on. The Philistines sent for Samson to make fun of him at the great feast of thanksgiving to their cruel god Dagon. But they didn't know who was coming. God was renewing Samson. Listen to his last prayer:

'Sovereign Lord, remember me again O God, please strengthen me just one more time. With one blow let me pay back the Philistines for the loss of my two eyes.'[2]

God heard – he couldn't change the past. But Samson was giving God the mess he had made and saying, 'God use it if you can.'

The answer came, 'I can – and I will.'

The strength of heaven flooded into him. Listening to the jeers of the enemies of God's people, he gripped the two centre pillars of the temple of Dagon. Never again would they laugh at Samson, or his God. He prayed once more,

'Let me die with the Philistines.'

Then he bowed his shoulders for the last time. Full power poured through the muscles. The pillars collapsed. The roof caved in on all the Philistine leaders and people that were there. He killed more enemies in his death than in all his life. What a man – and a tragedy that he only became what he should have been at the very end. But in his final triumph he points forward to Jesus, whose greatest victory was achieved in apparent failure and death.

STILL THE SAME OLD STORY

Samson was not the last leader in Israel to struggle with issues like sex, insecurity, lack of approval, and identity. That's not surprising. These are rooted in the imperfection of our humanity – our fallenness. In the early church, leaders and people had similar struggles, and Church history since then is full of such battles. The fact is, even with God's indwelling power we are still not perfected. Each of us is like a walking civil war, wanting to do God's will but struggling with desires pulling us in the opposite direction. What is God's answer to the problem? More rules? We know they don't work. Try harder? Works for a while – then we crash and burn.

His answer comes out of left field, as Americans say. To our religious mindset, Grace and Love are counter-intuitive.

But consider this question. What's the difference between King Saul and King David? Or between Peter and Judas? Simple! Like Saul and Judas, both David and Peter rebelled and betrayed their God. But unlike Saul and Judas they repented and were instantly, outrageously forgiven, cleansed and restored to their places in God's purposes. Saul spoke his own epitaph, 'I have been a fool and have gone sadly wrong', then fell on his own sword. Judas said, 'I have sinned by betraying innocent blood', went out and hanged himself. Remorse is self-centred and alienating. Repentance brings us under God's judgement which has fallen in fullness on Jesus. So it brings us into **instant** cleansing and restoration.

What a God! A Father of infinite mercy and grace.

When we don't life in the reality of the Spirit, we will live in the emptiness of materialism. Sometimes, aching, we may grasp at people using them for our consolation. Or we will grab at money and things. When we are spiritually and morally dead, emotionally exhausted and physically debauched, things still whisper 'I offer guaranteed repeatable experience.' How stupid to live for a 3D TV. A lady I knew said to me, 'We bought the biggest and best TV, Eric. It's worth spending out on one when you get to our age. **After all, it's our life now.**' The biggest obscenity of our age is the extent to which our lives are dominated by the acquisition of things, and the consumption of needless food.

THE KING WHO WAS A FOOL

Pride sits so easily with materialism. Things serve our selfishness, without any involvement in relationship. Material things enable us to arrange our surroundings so we are comfortable, always affirming our importance. Is that why we get so furious when the car won't start? After years of living like this we may be thoroughly infected by pride but still be religious. We can be a minister, a church officer, a deacon, an elder, a prophet, an evangelist or a member of the church council. Pride is so respectable – often surfacing in church relationships. It can turn the gateway to heaven into something like an anteroom of hell. At such moments Jesus must weep over his Church.

We may not be serving God at all, but may still think we are. That's frightening. Such service will not last one second in the radiance of the holy God. He is a consuming fire. The outshining of his purity, love and truth will burn up all that is not made by him.[3]

THE COMMITMENT WE MUST MAKE

May God grant to us the power of his Holy Spirit, so that all we are and do may endure the radiation of his holiness, being made of truth, love and Spirit – the very stuff of heaven. Otherwise we face the pain of being saved 'through the flames': close to what Revelation calls 'hurt by the second death'. The promise is that if we will commit ourselves to the Lord through all suffering, pain and persecution, we shall not be hurt by the second death. All that is selfish and hell-bound in us will be purged by walking through fire with him.

Without a sense of our special destiny we won't have the strength to fight sexual lust, the love of things and pride. We could end up being disqualified for the prize.

Why not take a few moments to survey the areas of life we have looked at – then claim the cleansing power of the death of Jesus?

> 'Lord by your blood clean me
> from lusts of the flesh,
> the love of things and pride.
> By your death liberate me
> from their power.
> Reign in me.
> By your resurrection
> wake me up.
> Above all,
> don't let me become useless.
> I will not serve any other master.
> Jesus, you are my Lord.
> Amen.'

So many people get it wrong. How do we get it right? It's the 'how' we now want to look at.

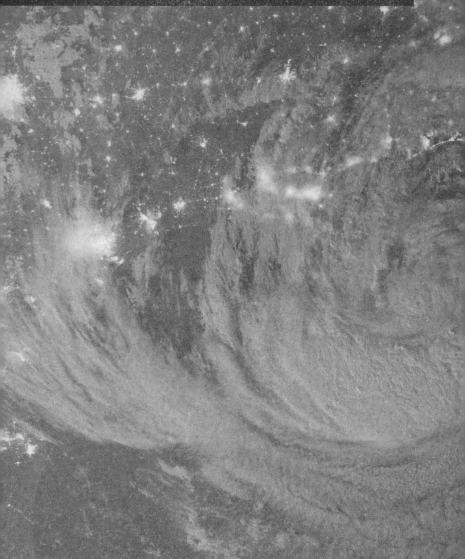

CHAPTER 4

DARKNESS RAGING
- DAYSTAR RISING

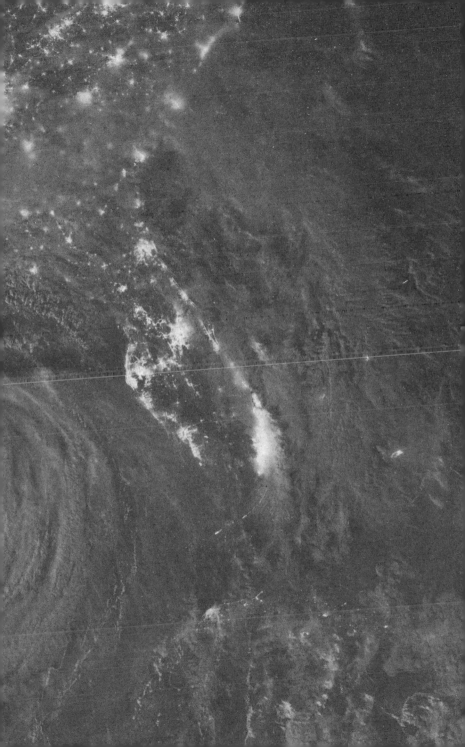

'Now this is not the end.
It is not even the beginning of the end.
But it is perhaps the end of the beginning.'[1]

HUMAN BEINGS – IMAGE AND LIKENESS OF GOD

In the beginning... God created. But it was not simply what we think of as an 'artistic' impulse. It came from the constant interplay of relationship between the Everlasting Father, the eternal Son and the Holy Spirit. It's the way the Trinity works. Love draws them into an ongoing dance of relationship – a kind of creative conversation constantly generating new ideas, bubbling with laughter, fizzing with fresh imagination. It is an eternal unfolding of creative activity, because he is the **living** God. Nothing static, dead or boring about him!

When his people are static, dead or boring they have ceased to reflect his nature. The name 'Yahweh' given to Moses as God's name thousands of years ago bears this out. Usually translated as 'I am what I am', its meaning is clearer as 'I am becoming what I am becoming'. He is limitless, constantly revealing more of what he is and what he is becoming. Unveiling his endlessly diverse personality is what the creation, especially the making of the human race, is all about.

'Then God said, "Let us make human beings in our image,
to be like us"'[2]

This is clear. People are to be the revelation of God. So the truth about humans is that we were made, men and women, to be the truth about God.

> *'So God created human beings in his own image, in the image of God he created him; make and female he created them.'*[3]

'Male' and 'female' describe sexual roles. It is hard for us as products of the world after the great rebellion in Eden, to understand what sex must have been before it. Our view of sex is horribly perverted. But we know this: it reflects God's concern that humans should not be alone. It expresses the self-sacrificing, permanent and total commitment which makes two people 'one flesh'.

> *'A man shall leave his father and his mother and hold fast to his wife and they shall become one flesh. And the man and his wife were both naked, and were not ashamed.'*[4]

Now the story of humanity becomes personal – it puts on the faces of a man and woman. Whatever your opinions about evolution, special creation, or modified evolutions; here the general becomes particular. We meet an individual, Adam, and know that he is 'special', and we view Eve the mother of the race; and wish we could have seen them in their innocence and splendour before rebellion and downfall.

THE DREAM OF HUMAN LOVE

Look at the description of their relationship – 'they were both naked'. That word 'naked' is huge. There were no barriers, no fear of strength, no despising of weakness. But a mutual enjoyment of beauty, giving and receiving of honour and right worship. Different in function yet equals in status, because the terrible barrier that would come between them after the rebellion was not then known. Theirs was a joining of body, mind and spirit that went down to the depths of their beings. Perfect union. All untainted by guilt. *'They were not ashamed.'*

'Shame' is terrible. It speaks of the awful guilt that we all feel: guilt for what we have done, guilt for what we should have done, guilt for what our race has done. Shame is guilt recognised as mine. But they felt none of it, they were free. When Adam first looked on Eve and rejoiced in the perfection of her breasts and the beauty of her hair he was not a voyeur. When she rejoiced in the worship of his eyes and the strength of his thighs she was not debased. They knew the reality of what we dream of when we 'fall in love'. Together they were beginning the revelation of the Creator God that was to come through humankind.

The God revealed in the image is strangely three-cornered, for out of their union was to come offspring. Here is one of the first hints of God as Trinity.

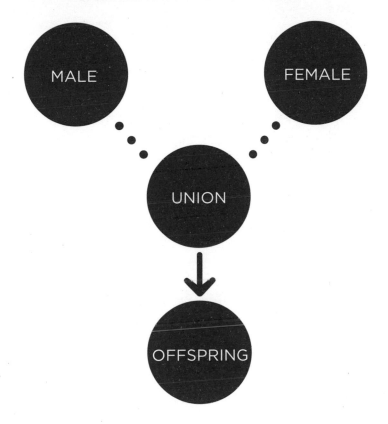

TO BE TRULY HUMAN, WE MUST CHOOSE

They were flawless, perfect but not yet perfected. Something remained undetermined. They were made in the image of God and no one ever yet bound the Creator. They had to be free, if they were to reveal the character of the living God. But they could never fully reveal him unless inhabited by Him. God is unique. He is himself. He has no equals – but he is love; and love never forces the beloved. That would deny and destroy love itself.

Only Adam and Eve could make the choice that would join them and their heirs to the living God for ever. The tree of life stood in the centre of the garden – but there was the enemy. The Father would not deny his children the right to hear Satan and choose his way if they wanted. So the tree of knowing good and evil was there with God's warning, 'Do not touch it. The day you do, you will die.'

Where does Satan come from? Certainly he is one of God's high creations, fallen, twisted, and perverted beyond recall. God's plan is to make us humans in *His* image, to carry and radiate God's glory to all creation. Most likely this intention triggered the Devil's rebellion. As Lucifer – the Lightbearer of God – he felt ousted from his position, pride burst out, he fell. Pure spirit in rebellion, he can never be redeemed. He now hates God. He planned to defile humankind and use us as a tool in his ambition to take the throne of the universe. From there he would turn heaven into an everlasting, cosmic torture chamber.

Once he carried the Light. Now Darkness raged in him. He offered Eve insight, knowledge and Godlike power. He lied. But she was deceived partly because she wanted to be. Yet the situation was not beyond hope. Deceived, Eve had disobeyed, but the image was a partnership. Adam's choice was crucial. It would destroy or redeem it. When he looked at Eve, how did he feel? Did he feel the huge void, the distance between them, and unknown before, the pain of loneliness? Did he hope that by joining her, he would be one with her again? Taking that fruit, he received the personal knowing of good and evil. Loneliness and darkness forever.

The light died, the music stopped, the spirit of God was ripped away, and death came. It is no good asking what would have been. We have no way of imagining what the world would have been if the choice had been the tree of life.

ADAM'S CHOICE - SATAN'S REIGN

In that moment this world was surrendered to Satan – he became the object of our worship, the tormentor of our desires, the master of our reactions. The whole world was exposed to his rule.

God knew – how could he not? In the moment of darkest tragedy he made a promise or rather a threat to Satan:

> 'I will put hostility between you and the woman, and between your offspring and her offspring; he will strike your head, and you will strike his heel.'[5]

It was the first promise that a redeemer would come to rescue humanity. But that was far in the future. Estrangement entered human life like poison. God had predicted, it meant alienation from ourselves, each other and the natural world. Though all seemed hopeless, the physical earth remained in its marred harmony and beauty still a testimony to the wonder of its maker.

Made for God, humanity was hungry for something to fill the emptiness, and sometimes fooled by Satan with false gods or fraudulent satisfactions. Still some refused to be deceived, thirsting for the real God whom they were sure was there, invisible but real.

Down long years of darkness, God's heart of fatherly love followed his wayward children. He answered those who called, while he called everyone. The promise of the offspring, the deliverer, grew stronger and clearer.

Abraham and his wife Sarah became a family, a tribe, a nation, and a great people. Still the Father worked to win the **hearts** of the people. Centuries passed; Covenant, Law, Judges, Kings, Rebellions, Rival Kingdoms, Prophets, Exiles, Return. Empires rose and fell. Finally Rome took centre stage. The Father was ready.

GOD'S ACTION,
THE LAST PROPHET OF THE OLD COVENANT

Zechariah was tired, old and tired. The two companion priests had left him, solitary in the Holy Place. The veil before him hid the Holy of Holies – where God's throne rested – the earthly seat of the heavenly King. The light of the seven-branched lampstand gleamed on the golden altar. Zechariah spread the incense upon live coals and waited until it kindled, smoke billowed, and perfume ascended. He bowed, and in that moment his world was upended, changed, and remade.

He knew it was an angel. The wind that blew the messenger's hair did not come from the curtained stillness of the Temple. The light that shone from him was purer and brighter than any sunrise Zechariah had ever seen. But years of unanswered prayer had dulled his faith. The news that his prayers were answered, that barren Elizabeth would bear a son who would himself be the forerunner of the Messiah seemed unbelievable – even from Gabriel. He said so, and paid for it with nine months of silence. Struck dumb, he would only speak after he had given the child the name John – gift of God.

What a man he grew to be! Something wild, glorious and free lived in him from birth. John was holy; but not with the bleak icy holiness of those who carefully calculated the merits of a tealeaf given to God. His was the high holiness of life in love with the Lord. 'The Baptist' they called him, because his burning heart was never satisfied till people were dipped in the river Jordan as a sign of repentance and forgiveness. He was the herald of the one to come. In the hour before the dawn when Christ the sun of God's goodness rose over the scene, John the Baptist blazed incandescent and thousands rejoiced in his light.

MARY'S CHOICE – GOD'S SON COMES

What of the beautiful girl who was to be the mother of the promised offspring? Six months after Zechariah emerged from the Temple, his eyes filled with a vision of living holiness, she met the same messenger – in Nazareth. There is a beauty about her, even now, as we read her story first written nineteen hundred years ago – the serenity, joy and radiance of a girl who has learned to walk with her God. Not even Gabriel breaching the veil that hides heavenly reality from earthly shadows could make her afraid. Only the seeming extravagance of his greeting troubled her. As the proclamation of the great King to come from her womb is made, she accepts his divine origin, his royal destiny and the eternity of his reign. She only asked one question. 'How will this happen?'

> *'The Holy Spirit will come upon you, and the power of the Most High will overshadow you. So the baby to be born will be holy, and he will be called the Son of God.'*[6]

All the sweet, wild, holy power of God pours into her in those words. With quiet grace and calm this teenage girl ponders the will of the Father; knowing it will mean small-town gossip, scandal and the life-long ruin of her reputation. The long history of the Trinity's loving and planning all trembled in the balance of this young girl's answer. How gentle is our God. *'Here am I the servant of the Lord. Let it be with me according to your word.'* All of heaven must have exploded with joy at those words. The promise was fulfilled. The ever-living son, the Word, the outshining of the all-creating God, became a single cell in his own creation – an ovum in the womb of a woman. The Word became flesh. The Daystar was rising.

JESUS' CHOICE – THE KINGDOM COMES

He called himself *'son of man'*, knowing some would not understand – and others understanding would be outraged. The title dated from the time of Daniel. Some said the son of man would be the Messiah, others – the ideal human, still others – the righteous redeemer. Apparently nobody thought all of them could be true! Adam's choice had been, 'my will not God's'. Jesus was the first human to live out: *'Not my will but yours'*. Paul called him the second Adam, the beginner of a new race born to live as he lived; spiritually alive, holy and free.

The 'good news of the kingdom of God' was constant in all his preaching. Jesus had come to announce the lifting of Satan's long domination. He could say *'the kingdom of God is among you'* because he stood among them – the demonstration of that kingdom. To the scribes and Pharisees, incessantly seeking for new minutiae of ritual law with which to bind everyone including themselves, he was a menace. Not that he was a law breaker; he simply lived so high above and beyond the law that it was irrelevant. That annoyed them, particularly when it interfered with the smooth ritual of synagogue services.

JESUS' CHOICE – RELEASE TO RELIGIOUS CAPTIVES

Eighteen years is a long time to be bent almost double with curvature of the spine. Sitting in the synagogue listening to the young rabbi on this Sabbath, the woman's pain was worse than usual so she couldn't lift her eyes to see him. Then people around her gasped. He was calling her from the women's section of the synagogue. Then she was standing right before him. He spoke with quiet authority: 'Lady, you are freed from your illness.' Hands touched her head with gentle power, immediately a demonic tension was banished. Muscles regained their old strength and normal position. Her spine straightened, she stood upright and praised. She would have understood the lines beloved by Martin Luther King: 'Free at last, free at last. Praise God almighty, I'm free at last'.

The synagogue president and his cronies were furious. 'Disgusting. Get healed during the week, not on a Sabbath.' Eyes that had warmed her with compassion now flashed with hidden fire. 'Actors! You would untie a donkey to water it on the Sabbath. Isn't it right to untie this daughter of Israel, bound by Satan for eighteen years, **on the Sabbath.**' They had no answer and slunk away in shame.

I heard of one man in Devon who could have joined them. Each Sunday he would stand up in church to pray, 'Oh Lord, we've been caught in the webs of sin, Satan has ensnared us…' It continued week after week. One Sunday a forthright character decided he'd had enough of it. The prayer began as usual. At the end of the first sentence a stentorian voice boomed out, 'Oh Lord, **kill that spider!**'

JESUS' CHOICE – 'NOT MY WILL'

That's what Jesus came to do: to rob the spider of life and power. The proclamation and the miracles were part of it, but the battleground where the victory had to be won was inside him. As his popularity with the great mass of people levelled off, so enemies within the political and religious establishment began to push forward. The plotters surrounded Jesus with spies and *agents provocateurs*. The atmosphere was filled with suspicion and intrigue. Yet he loved them. He answered their dangerous questions with courtesy and honesty, and constantly amazed them with replies that turned their tiny worlds upside down.

The cross had always stood as a dark shape on the edge of his consciousness. Now as time grew shorter and the moment drew nearer, the full horror of it crystallised. Hearing the easy triumphalism of the apostles, Jesus tried to prepare them. Time and again he described what would happen to him. But they couldn't hear him. They rejected such thoughts. Even on the way to the Last Supper they were still arguing over the distribution of cabinet posts in Jesus' new world government.

At the Passover Supper not one of them was able to humble himself to wash the feet of Jesus and the others. It was a terrifying measure of their failure to absorb even a tiny part of the teaching he had given over three years. Still more painful to him, in his love for them, was the confident boasting of their loyalty.

'You will betray me,' he said.

'We will never let you down, even if we should die with you. '

'These others may fall away, I never will.'

The demons must have laughed, and taunted Jesus, jeering at his manifest failure.

Jesus' last attempt to reach Judas failed. Running from the truth Judas went out into the night and never saw light again. All the disciples would betray, desert and deny him; Peter worst of all. The agony he felt was partly for them: he loved them.

JESUS' CHOICE – 'YOUR WILL BE DONE'

Jesus was alone as no-one ever was, though not yet abandoned by the Father. As he knelt in the garden the issue was still the same. Would a man, made of flesh and blood like Adam, willingly stand in a wicked world and reverse Adam's choice, saying, 'God I love you for yourself. I want your will not my own'? There in Gethsemane he faced the cross, and battle was joined between good and evil.

Fiery torches in the garden, a traitor's kiss, a beating-up, bloody fists, jeering laughter, gobbets of spit, hate-filled faces, cowardly judges, a cynical king – Jesus was silent. He said no word, because to speak would have been to pile more guilt against them. He went on loving them.

Through three Jewish trials, the only time he spoke was when the High Priest left his judge's seat, beside himself with rage, shrieking in the face of Jesus, *'In the name of the living God I now put you on oath: Tell us if you are the Messiah, the son of God?'*

He replied calmly, levelly, unafraid. *'I am, and you shall see the son of man sitting at the right hand of the Almighty and coming on the clouds of heaven.'*

It was what they had waited for. 'Blasphemy!' they shouted with delight. Religious hatred had triumphed.

PILATE'S CHOICE – GO WITH THE FLOW

He went on loving them. When handed over to the Roman Governor he said nothing. Poor Pilate, vain, weak and a bully; politically inept, intellectually no match for those clever men Annas and Caiaphas, he tried to be a 'noble Roman'. Unfortunately he was shallow and heavy handed, compensating for his lack of subtlety by unwise use of force. He tried to save Jesus Christ. He failed.

Stripped naked, stretched tight and tied to a pillar, Jesus was scourged. Leather thongs bearing pieces of bone, and metal flailed his back ripping off strips of skin, then flesh and muscle fibre. There was no legal limit to the number of blows. It only stopped when the man with the scourge was exhausted. They mocked him as 'A King', crowning him with a circlet made from thorns like great nails.

In all this, never forget the scheme of the enemy. God had emptied himself of power and been made a man. Satan saw his greatest opportunity. The steady erosion of popularity, the turning back of many disciples, the hatred of the authorities and the desertion and betrayal by the apostles were all part of his assault on the psychology of the man. Then, utterly alone, Jesus had to face the physical agony and the spiritual desolation.

Nine o'clock in the morning. They nailed the right hand first, then the left. A loop of rope round the legs pulled down hard, a nail through the ankles. Then the cross lifted high, was dropped into its socket in the ground.

JESUS' CHOICE – 'LOVE YOUR ENEMIES'

Every bone in the upper torso snapped out of joint yet... *'Father forgive them they do not know what they are doing.'* He went on loving.

Muscles strained, ligaments tore, empty sockets grated – and still the heart pumped life round the obscenely distended body. The cleverest twist of Satan's knife was the coming of his mother. Still beautiful, serene in her trust, she was to receive today the *'sword to pierce your own heart'* promised by Simeon years ago in the Temple.

'Lady, go home with John; John, treat her as your mother.'

Gently, courteously, he was telling her, 'I am not coming home.' Lovingly truth-telling, he broke her heart.

Just before midday one of the thieves fell silent – the other continued babbling curses. Then the quiet one rebuked his companion. 'We are getting what we deserve. He has done no wrong... Jesus, remember me when you come as King.' After three hours of insult that is quite a request.

'I promise you, today you will be with me in Paradise.' What a man! What a glorious man! If in such extreme pain he could love someone who had treated him so badly, then his love was the out-shining radiance of God. It still is.

JESUS' CHOICE – OBEY GOD AT ALL COSTS

Twelve o'clock, midday. Darkness descended – a darkness to frighten people. Whatever its cause, it continued for three hours. In those hours, the Father apparently reached backward and forward in human history to take the very essence of each one of us and place it in Christ. Jesus received us, identified with us, became one with us. He accepted our dark side, our sin. So in the darkness the Father accused his son of sin: every sin, and every consequence; sickness, disease, torture, famine, war, divorce, rape, drug addiction, abuse and death. Every nasty, filthy, deceitful, greedy, shameful trick – whether hidden or open, committed in word, thought or deed, all our defilements were piled on him.

Now filthy with our sin, rotten and stinking in the nostrils of a holy God, he was fitted no longer for heaven but for hell. In this awful moment the relationship between the everlasting Father and the eternal son was ripped apart; and the son fell away, down, down in the abyss. Grinning shallowness, cruel idiocy, rapacious nothingness closed around him. The King of heaven languished – a captive in hell. For a moment.

'My God, my God, why have you abandoned me?' The cry of desolation echoed round the hills, no answer came, none was

possible. It was the loneliest moment ever. It was for you and me. The ransom was paid. He had paid the price of our release from Satan's clutches.

JESUS' OBEDIENCE – GOD'S VICTORY

Satan had failed! In the moment of seeming victory he had lost. The grinding pressure he had applied to the son of man had provoked no sin, selfishness, or rage, and exposed no pride – only love. Satan, whose only right was to hold the guilty in his kingdom, had slain the innocent.

'I *thirst,*' Jesus said, but wanted nothing they could give him. Thirst is the perpetual state of hell. He had plumbed its depths, but nothing could hold him there. The account was fully paid. So even now echoing down the centuries, we still hear the great cry, '*It is accomplished*'. He dumped our degradation, filth and guilt, and began to rise.

The innocent Maker had died for his guilty creations, and henceforth any of them could claim his sacrifice for their release. From that moment in our space and time, I was forgiven – and so were you. We only need to receive him: life for life, loyalty for loyalty. Accept him and we change sides in life's great war.

GOD'S VICTORY - HUMANS REMADE

Breathing *'Father, into your hands I commit my Spirit'*, Jesus surrendered the life he had put on in the womb, and rose into the full glory of the heavenly realm. Because he did, we can find new life. Born again, we step into his kingdom - the kingdom of God's dear son. We live in this world as he did, in the plan of the Father, in the will of the King. So we discover the truth of what Jesus said: *'I said, you are gods... to whom the word of God came'.* [7] Humans like gods - at last! The soldiers saw he was dead, but decided to check. To make sure, they pierced his side with a spear. Blood and water came out. That not only proved his death, but makes it almost certain he died of a ruptured heart. What a portrait God gives of himself: nail-pierced, thorn-crowned, heart-broken. Truly, **God is love.**

By the sacrifice of Jesus we are loosed from the chains of guilt, released from the dungeon of our despair, and set free to live, by love, the life which God planned for us from eternity. That purpose has never changed. God still loves you and wants you to live for him in a way no one else ever could. The cross of Calvary has made it possible for you to enter your destiny and really live.

OUR CHOICE - TO BE MADE NEW

Given the foulness of sin, and the glory of God's holiness; the love that took Jesus from the heights of heaven to the depths of hell to rescue us, must be enormous. He was so determined you should accomplish your purpose. Let's gladly give thanks.

The following prayer may help:

> 'Lord Jesus Christ, as I look at your cross
> I am amazed at your love.
> You didn't have to do it.
> But you died for me, for all of us.
> I worship you as perfect man and loving God.
> Thank you for taking my faults
> into your body on the cross.
> I give you my sin, stupidity, guilt and failure.
> Thank you for forgiving me,
> for making me clean, for setting me free.
> Thank you. Thank you.
> Help me to walk always in the
> cleansing light of your sacrifice.
> Amen.'

For many people the story of Calvary is the whole gospel; but it's not – it is the doorway to the real thing. The Lord has opened the door, so let's go right in...

CHAPTER 5
DISCIPLESHIP
– ANYTHING
CAN HAPPEN

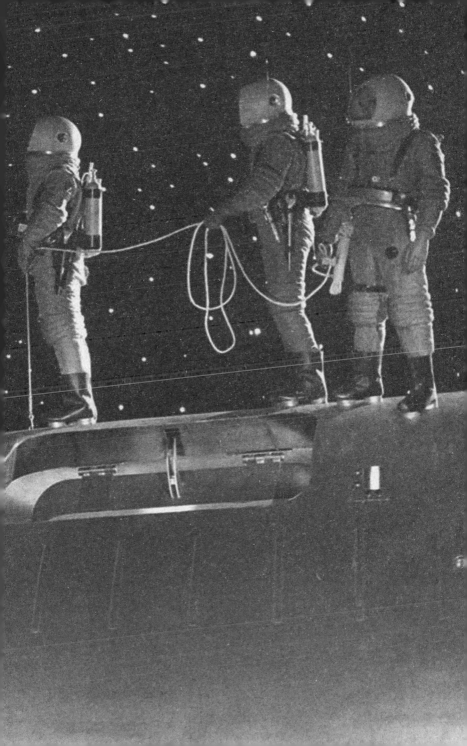

SERVING THE LIVING LORD –
IN THE POWER OF THE SPIRIT

When my kids were young we often watched the classic TV puppet series' Stingray and International Rescue. Stingray began with a Hollywood epic voice that snarled, 'Anything can happen in the next half-hour!'

It was rarely true, of course. Usually the adventures of the 'life-like' puppets were comfortably predictable – like church? At least, that is the way we seem to want it!

'What happened at church this morning?'

'Oh, nothing much, the same as usual.'

That conversation should be impossible. For with God **nothing** is impossible. Something must happen and almost anything could. 'All things are possible.' As C. S. Lewis put it in the Narnia books, 'Aslan is not a tame lion'. We deal with the **living** God, and because he lives, we should live also. But so often we allow circumstances, our own digestions or satanic pressure to rob us of his presence. Like the two on the road to Emmaus, we walk heads bowed, voices low and faces downcast. Gloom trails behind us. We almost deserve to be called *'of all men most miserable'*! Jesus still asks as he did then,

'What are you talking about, as you walk along?'

The sadness showed as they looked at him! 'You must be the only man in Jerusalem who doesn't know what's been happening.'

'What?' he asked.

Their pain was clear as they talked about the innocent one, condemned and slaughtered by a cynical alliance between Jewish religion and Roman power. Then the dead man not allowed to rest decently in his tomb, the grave opened, strange messengers and hysterical women. Men were sent to investigate but *'him they did not see'*. They were talking about the right story, but from a mistaken perspective: the collapse of hope.

His viewpoint was the joy-filled triumph of God's purpose. 'Brainless and slow-hearted. Don't you see? It was **necessary** for the Christ to suffer that way and to enter into his splendour.' He took them to the beginning, to Adam, then a lightning tour through the Old Testament. Overturning all their petty and earthbound thinking, he showed them the mighty plan of God and 'Christ the Tiger' in the centre of it. He reset their Jewish frame in its cosmic context.

How long did it take to walk those seven miles: three, maybe four hours? They understood. Excitement gripped them. Yet not till he broke the bread in the house did they recognise him. Then he was gone.

WE WALK IN THE POWER OF THE HOLY SPIRIT

Now watch them dash back to Jerusalem, run up the steps, burst into the upper room, and start to say, 'We've seen him! Jesus is alive,' only to be met by, 'We know! Peter's seen him.' Glorious anti-climax! They were transformed. They had met the resurrection Christ. But by his direct command they were prevented from going out to tell anybody. He planned a gospel bigger than just **talking** about his own resurrection. The good news they were to proclaim was the sharing of his resurrection, and they couldn't do this until they'd experienced the reality. 'Wait' he said, 'until power from above comes down upon you... In a few days you will be baptised in the Holy Spirit.'

Quick! Form ranks in party lines! Back to the trenches! Theological grenades at the ready: Fire!

Pentecostal!
　Liberal!
　　Experientialist!
　　Doctrinalist!
　　Modernist!
　　　Traditionalist!
　　　Charismatic!
　　　Dead religionist!

Well, now we have dispensed with the formalities perhaps we can think about the phrase. After all, something the Bible reports as said by John the Baptist four times[1], Peter[2], Paul[3] and Jesus himself[4] cannot be all bad!

Baptism: To the Greeks the simple act of dipping anything in water or other liquid so that it is thoroughly saturated – sometimes a shirt in a bowl of dye. Used by the Jews to describe the act of repentance when someone was dipped in a river or lake to publicly admit his sin and need of God's cleansing. Christians took it over and filled it with more meaning.

WE LIVE IN THE FULLNESS OF THE HOLY SPIRIT

It was the moment of change, the moment when a person was buried with Christ, and raised in the power of his resurrection. The old lifestyle of independent action was laid in the grave, and the new life in the Holy Spirit was established. Death to the old man, life from Jesus Christ.

Four rivers flowed out of Eden, their names giving a beautiful description of a river of life: Freely Flowing, Stream, Arrow-Swift, Bursting with Sweetness. Ezekiel later saw a river flowing from the Temple. Wherever it went new life came. First it was ankle deep, then knee deep, thigh deep and finally *deep enough to swim in'*. Jesus promised us *'rivers of living water'* which John said was the gift of the Holy Spirit.

Do you see it? The Holy Spirit of God is the fountain of God's life. It pours out of him bubbling and effervescent, then streams into us. This wild, sweet, river is a person of beauty, splendour, glory and divine authority. He is the agent and proof of the resurrection. We give Christmas presents, but Jesus gives us an Easter/Ascension present – his spirit as our share in his triumph.[5]

If you are in Christ, the Spirit of God is yours! But the reality of the experience may be held back; firstly because you have not understood that he is given freely.

> *'How much more will the heavenly Father give the Holy Spirit to those who ask him!'*[6]

Maybe you have never reached out and **received** by faith what is already given. God wants to make the blessings he has promised, real to you. Now, the Holy Spirit is the Lord. If you don't go on obeying him you will fail to know his fullness. This is essential to being filled with the Holy Spirit. However, nobody's perfect yet. We all fail in obedience. So we need to learn to repent – fast. This is the other key to fullness.

WE LIVE IN OBEDIENCE TO THE HOLY SPIRIT

So, 'Baptism in the Spirit' must at least mean being buried and raised again in the Spirit. Its reality will not come until we surrender the inner fortress of our will, to the God-sized authority of the Holy Spirit.

Such a moment may or may not be a great crisis. It might come with great emotional explosions; whatever, it will be a moment when the sovereign God enters and takes over from the false sovereign – 'me'. At last the river of God's life begins to flow into, through and out of a human being – and we are back to the original dream of Eden. Though we're fallen creatures in a fallen world, we have begun to really live by eating from the tree of life.

As we move in obedience to the Holy Spirit, the Father starts unfolding the pattern of his destiny for us. Living under his Lordship we are free! Like a bird in the air, a fish in the water or a horse on the open downs, we are free because a man or a woman living in the Spirit is living in his or her natural element.

'Now the Lord is the Spirit and where the Spirit of the Lord is, There is freedom.'[7]

This is not freedom to sin but freedom to do God's will; to find his plan and live it out, a life that is pure, holy and disciplined. It's not because a law says I ought to be those things. It's because I know my destiny is to be like Jesus. The Holy Spirit within me, draws me towards the will of God and gives me power to live it.

THE ALTERNATIVE – TO LIVE IN BONDAGE

Those who will not live in this relationship are doomed to live under life-denying Laws, with rules and regulations constantly proliferating as people seek to explain them more fully. The result is people that are bound up, tensed up, and miserable, barren, powerless, and stereotyped, under judgement and judgemental. Or, we can decide that keeping so many rules is impossible, and start to live in a phoney freedom; phoney because whatever gives me the right to sin brings me into terrible bondage. Useless and spiritually dull I become a walking advertisement for Christian boredom.

I was meant for better things. I am a child of God, not a robot. A robot functions automatically according to a set of predetermined instructions. But the child of a loving Father is free. Free to laugh, to cry, free to feel joy and anger within the Father's arms. The emotions are released, because in the trusting relationship with the Father, a child can expose all the pains, hurts, rage, joys, bitterness, excitements and agonies of their heart. Happy the man or woman who lives like this. A deep, secure happiness comes from knowing we have shown the severest hurts and the very worst in us to God – and he still loves us. Because this is true freedom, it is dangerous. We have the right to participate in God's purpose for us. However, we also have the right to disobey, to get out of God's plan. Thus many stagnate and die respectably. As an American clergyman said at a funeral: 'Brothers and sisters, this corpse has been a member of this church for forty years'! If you are one of those asleep in Christ, then 'Wake up. Wake up sleeper. Rise from the dead. Christ waits to bless you with Light.'

Alternatively, we can backslide into spectacular disobedience, and force God to let us learn the truth of the phrase 'miserable as sin'.

THE ROAD HOME – REPENTANCE

Maybe you have done that already and are reading this in a 'far-off country'. Listen to God's voice. "My child, my plan for you is not static and immovable. It is dynamic and flexible. Simply surrender to me your mistakes – your stupidity, your sin. My grace is greater. I am able to incorporate it into my plan, so that finally it will cover you with my glory. Only give it **all** to me."

The only voice that tells you, 'It's all over. You've really blown it. You'll never be any good as a Christian now,' is Satan's. The Father sees you even a long way away. The moment you start to come home he runs to meet you, flings his arms around you and holds you. You have made some wrong choices – give them to him. Surrender 'second best' in repentance to him and he will work on it. He will forge it into 'best' in the white heat of his love.

As a child of God called to a destiny that is yours alone, you have to be aware of Satan's power to use 'the enemy within'. You **cannot** be defeated by any power from outside. When an impregnable fortress is locked securely against an enemy, the clever attacker gets a traitor inside to open the doors – and Satan is clever.

A young trainee minister was preaching a sermon before the Principal of his college, C. H. Spurgeon. Firmly he expounded Ephesians 6, about putting on the armour of God. The helmet of salvation, breastplate of righteousness, shield of faith and all the other equipment was enthusiastically donned. Then he asked with ringing rhetoric:

'And now where are you, Satan?'

Spurgeon leaned forward over the balcony and shouted, 'Inside the armour.'

THE UNHOLY TRINITY

Inside us Satan finds an unholy trinity of weakness where too often he receives ready welcome:

- Misuse of sex (lust)
- Love of things/money (materialism)
- Self-centredness (pride)

If you don't want him to rob you of the crown that Jesus waits to give you, you must fight against his control in these areas.

The Holy Spirit – the power of Jesus' resurrection – is given to make you holy, a true disciple. Holiness and discipline begin with understanding that God has a special purpose that will never be fulfilled if not by you.

(i) Lust: If God has planned for you to meet and marry a certain person, you do not have the right to deprive that person of the blessing of your love (doubtful blessing though you may feel it to be!). Don't give yourself to someone else. Remember too, sex is made to happen inside marriage. Marriage is a commitment designed by God to protect **sex**, because he wants us to enjoy it! Sex used as passing entertainment turns sour, scars and destroys our real humanity. Research indicates sex outside of marriage between people who love each other and intend to marry, is destructive of their present relationship and future stability. If the person you love is intended for you from eternity, then demonstrate your love for them by enduring the pain of waiting – **that** will prove that you love them!

Sex is powerful, and needs a strong purpose-built container – marriage. Enjoyed in marriage it becomes the glue that holds a couple in growing tenderness that gets better and better.

'How do I know who is right for me?' people ask. Answer: we can marry whoever we like provided they are single, in Christ and of the opposite sex. Look for someone seeking God's kingdom, the fullness of his Spirit, a coinciding of interests, growing friendship, and a meeting of mind and spirit. If we seek God and his kingdom, he will guide us by his Holy Spirit in us. He wants us to be happy. So he calls us to sexual purity. We'll never know the joy of chastity if we are not chaste. Your virginity is a marvellous gift from God, don't let anyone take it from you, and don't throw it away in a series of stupid sexual adventures. Marriage is the holy place where you yield that gift to the one for whom it is intended.

TRUE LOVE WAITS

Yeah, yeah, yeah! I know this is a high standard and to some, feels impossible. We must clearly understand the nature of personal destiny. You see, if God has plans for you and me, then we matter too much to throw it all away. Real love would only ask the loved one to do what is right. Can we ask someone for whom God has a special destiny and meaning, to defile that purpose – and say 'I acted in love'? No way, but we do. Christian or agnostic, in reflective moments we can recognise that the longing for gratification 'now' has often overwhelmed our knowledge of what is best for the relationship. We lost the individual. The person before us became a commodity, little more than a recreational facility. Purity in sexual relations turns on recognising the unique vital nature of each individual made in God's image. The way forward is to ask him for the **real** love that loves the other person too much to do what is wrong.

Jesus has encouragement for us. He knows how difficult it is to stand up for him and his words, in a sexually loose generation. So there are special blessings for those who do it – a clearer sense of identity, purpose and spiritual authority. Probably more of us are conscious of failure in this area than any other. I know what it is to try again and again, and to fail. There is only one answer. Confess your sin, receive forgiveness and go on. I want to encourage you because I've been there. I was once an adulterer. I know his Holy Spirit can make a dirty person clean. He did it for me. I was bound, helpless before my lust. Through years of struggle he sustained me, then set me free. 'Thank God'. No matter how often we fall, we are still called to purity. We don't have to live in bondage. So let's obey the King. We can **live in freedom.**

(ii) Materialism: As a natural expression of materialism, the love of things and money creeps up on us quietly and gradually. It is a good respectable sin fitting itself uniquely to working-class culture, middle-class preferences and upper crust indulgence. At its most noble it surfaces in the love of nature, especially in the artistic and in romantics. Swept along by the love of mountains and valleys, rivers, lakes, and beautiful views, they can easily make a god of nature.

Some environmentalists come close to this sort of idolatry, and for some Mother Earth is the only deity worth bothering with. They are mistaken. The earth and sky with all their wonders are meant to lead us in worship to the unseen God who is their author. Others who enjoy physical activities such as climbing, fell-walking or surfing may be led into a false dichotomy: 'I feel I can know God better out in the open air than sitting in a stuffy old church'. Understandable – and untrue. It will be true of certain occasions, but as a general principle it is simply a deception.

The earth was given to the human race to be held in trust. Adam was made steward of the earth, given dominion over it. It was to be a working relationship. He was not to worship it, but to wisely govern it as God's ambassador. The earth was made for us. We are to take care of it as our home. We are accountable for it. So we should never worship anything made from the earth, nor bow down to it; that's blasphemy. Our consumer society is blasphemous precisely because it is **thing-**centred.

Some people go to work, not to provide for families but to buy more things. Many of these agree to have no children because they don't want 'messy kids' spoiling their beautiful homes and possessions. Jesus called it *'serving mammon'*. It's easy for Christians to be swept along with the rest, in unspoken worship of the products of the electronic age. Powerful cars smoothly accelerating away from the opposition, huge HD 3D screens so vivid they are more real than real life, ovens that think for you, washing equipment that does everything except play 'Blue Danube', Sound Systems 'better than being there':

gadgets galore. Pay your money, bow down and worship – and die inside. With all their glitter, things bring disappointment as they date, bondage when they are threatened – and death when we are tied to them.

GOD'S GIFT, OUR PLEASURE

Nothing is bad in itself, and God richly gives all things for us to enjoy. And we will, provided we don't regard any possessions as ultimately ours. If we know they are gifts from God, then we will be free from them, truly able to enjoy them, and even accept it cheerfully when they get spoilt, broken or destroyed. In the end they don't really matter. Let's enjoy what God gives but hold our possessions loosely, so that when they are gone our hearts don't chase after them, but stay at home in God.

We are covetous, and generosity is not something that comes easily. Plus the financial crisis pressures us to be meaner than we have ever been. Even the Church has been affected. But we are called by an amazingly generous Heavenly Father to reflect his nature. So let's learn generosity, by giving money away till it hurts. Next time you are faced with a request for funds in the kingdom of God, dare to ask him what you should give. Assess each situation. Listen to him. Then give what he says – even if it seems too much! Giving your money away is your destiny and privilege. Few things are so exciting or liberating. It's a delightfully anarchistic thing to do in our greedy society!

The Government's steady demolition of our welfare system may make short-term fiscal sense. But when structures erected to care for the poor, weak, and sick are destroyed to save money for the prosperous, the message is clear – such people are disposable. Is that why some muggers seem to feel the old and sick are fair game?

We need to take collective action to challenge the selfish assumptions of our society. Initiatives like 'Christians Against Poverty' and Food Banks are showing the way forward. Time to join in?

(iii) Pride: What do we do about it? Sometimes it can be obvious. More often it is subtle and all the more dangerous. The fact is 'I' like reigning over 'my' life. Even when I know it's making me miserable I hang on, desperately trying to maintain my hold on the controls. Here the principle of individual destiny cuts right across my rebellion, and yours.

Without a clear sense of God's purpose, there is a grave danger that I will determine the way ahead on my own. That may feel alright, even for a Christian, but if I accept that God has a plan for each individual, the priority becomes the discovery of **his** will – not mine. The Spirit of God wrestles with my spirit to bring it into obedience to Christ because the king of kings wants me to reign in life. That can only happen when the Spirit of the King reigns in me. He confronts the rebellious heart and requests obedience. Once I submit (it may take a while!) he asks me to sit with him on the throne.

HUMILITY

Humility is rare but beautiful, the fruit of dependence and obedience. The only way to be truly humble and happy is to surrender freely to the Lord and to his destiny for me. I wasn't made to run my life on my own. Without his authority as King over me there is no authority in me. He is the most splendid conqueror the world has ever known. He wins by loving. Only he has earned the right to reign over me – or you. The scars in his hands, feet and side are his pledge to us of love that goes to hell and back. The wounded God who died of a broken heart because of his love for us, only has one desire: that we should be what we're meant to be – free.

WE LIVE IN THE FREEDOM OF THE SPIRIT

As his Holy Spirit pours through these areas cleansing and releasing them to his ideal, freedom will increasingly be ours. Freedom – not to sin, but to do what is right. Freedom to really live – the life of the risen Christ in us. This gives us hope of glory now and forever.

We will become our true selves. The adventure of God's own life will go out into the earth to reveal itself in our humanity. Each of us will know God differently from anyone else, and the revelation received will shine through us to be seen by others. Your life is an unrepeatable, priceless once-only work of art. You are an artist's original. Even the angels of high heaven are waiting to see that revelation of the Father's heart. You must live what no one ever lived before.

Don't let fear hold you back. The Lord is with you.

> '**Lord God,**
> **thank you for the**
> **privilege of being me.**
> **Give me the guts**
> **to take hold of your grace.**
> **Give me the courage**
> **to enter your creative holiness.**
> **Make me the person**
> **you want me to be.**
> **Amen.'**

Remember those words from *Star Trek*: 'To boldly go where no one has gone before'? That is your calling. And you have something far better than the 'Starship Enterprise'. You have the Lord of life, the Holy Spirit, in you. The power that raised Jesus from the dead in our space and time, and seated him on the throne of power in the eternal heavens, can certainly carry you 'where no one has gone before'. So boldly go…

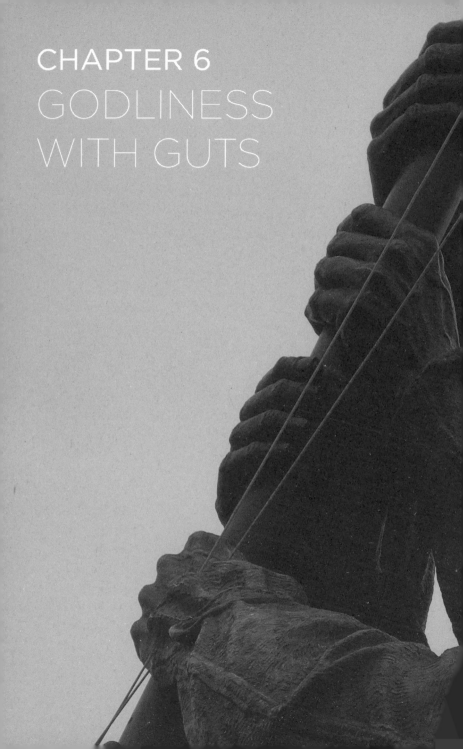

CHAPTER 6
GODLINESS
WITH GUTS

THE CALL TO COURAGE

The cripple was healed – no doubt about it! Whoops of joy filled the entrance, attracting a huge crowd as he danced and jumped his way up the steps into the Temple. Peter immediately took advantage of the scene by proclaiming the authority of Jesus the Christ once crucified, now risen from the dead. The priests were outraged, and Peter and John were soon arrested. After a night in the cells to cool them down, they were arraigned for trial before the whole Jewish establishment. But their ardour was not dampened. Totally undeterred, Peter the fisherman from Galilee set about putting them on trial instead: *'Jesus Christ of Nazareth **whom you crucified** has healed the man you now see before you.'* Astonished at such outspokenness by these uneducated common men (literally 'ungrammatical idiots!'), the priests thought that there was only one explanation for the boldness displayed by Peter and John – they had been with Jesus.

He had proved impossible to deal with. Now it seemed his followers would be like him! They had come away from their encounter with Jesus, convinced of the importance of the message, and certain of their own part in its proclamation. Peter knelt amongst an unbelievably large catch of fish and said, *'Go away from me, Lord, I am too sinful'*. Jesus did not deny Peter's sinfulness, only the conclusion he'd reached. 'Don't be afraid,' he said. It may seem to us that a sinful person dares too much, entering the service of God. It's worse for us to allow guilt-fuelled fear to stop us. Faith dares to trust the outrageous grace of God.

The people of the early church were men and women with a cause. They had a passion for Jesus and a vision for his Kingdom. Today, many of us have forgotten we have been personally commissioned by the risen Christ to carry his message into the world. We don't have to apologise for our presence, or our message; only for our ineffectiveness in demonstrating it. We should always tackle life and witness with joyful confidence, and sometimes aggressively – never timidly.

There is a place for the fighting spirit. Unfortunately, too often, we use it to fight each other. Meanwhile the battle for the relief of suffering and the proclamation of the gospel gets forgotten. Much preaching would also be hugely improved by an injection of aggression. We rarely hear preaching designed to send troops into war; with the idea that we are actually on the winning side, and our contribution is vital to victory. When we preachers make Jesus real – we give our audiences the heart of Christian courage.

JESUS, THE HUMAN FACE OF GOD

Earlier we looked at Jesus as a sort of weak, ineffective, even effeminate 'nice' man. More than anything else, this image is responsible for today's desperately low level of attainment among Christian men. We become what we worship. Therefore we must be sure that we worship the real Jesus – the authentic New Testament Christ.

He wasn't boring! The **common** people listened to him with delight. He made people chuckle with suggestions they could feed their sons on a lump of rock, or with a snake instead of a fish. His parody of the pompous, self-congratulations of a Pharisee at prayer made them roar with laughter. He raised a girl from the dead, then arranged for her to have something to eat. On an urgent journey he stopped to ask a smelly old lady to talk about her life story, including twelve years of illness, listened to her tale of woe then healed her. Compassion meant he refused to play up to a bunch of self-righteous, judgemental, religious hypocrites in the affluent house of Simon the leper. Instead, he accepted the clumsy, tearful, embarrassing repentance of a known prostitute. By doing so, he made enemies for life of those powerful men.

We must get back to the Jesus of the New Testament: the real man, the only real human being who ever lived, who sets the standard for us all. We must grasp the blood and guts reality of the incarnation. In too many churches there still seems to be a feeling that the Gospels are a source of pretty stories suitable for little children and women! Such an outdated attitude not only devalues women and children, it robs men of the chance to explore the mystery of manhood. Explaining the Bible, ministers need to keep Jesus as the keystone of their preaching – the living one who joins the elements of the written word of God into a unified revelation.

MANLY - NOT MACHO

If we are to become **manly** Christians, we men must study the Gospels. In the same way women can be liberated to be womanly warriors of Christ, by studying the man Jesus.

He was a man of courage and endurance beyond our normal notions. Having had his back reduced to living pain-wracked mincemeat, he still carried a heavy wooden cross halfway up a hill before finally collapsing. While enduring this, he carried on being what he was. He was not changed in essence by the torture – he was revealed by it. His reactions were the reactions of love. This was the integrity of true manhood. Knowing he was to die a hideous death, already maimed and reduced to something that no longer looked human; he could still turn to women weeping with sympathy, to say, 'Don't weep for me. Weep for yourselves.' He felt the pain that was coming on them in the future more than his own.

That's what it really means to be a **man**. To endure all things and then more, to go on and on into the darkness of death; through it, out into resurrection. This is real holiness – the boldness of a man set apart for God's purpose, and living it out. We won't learn it from anyone else but Jesus – and he wants to teach us, as we walk with him.

HAPPY AND HOLY

Jesus was unique. So was his life. It's the same with you. There is an area of life that can be touched by God's power only through **you**. The greatness of his power in you is immeasurable, its effectiveness only limited by your availability. He has given you power to enable you to live a holy life. You don't know what you can do. His eternal purpose is that you should be *'Whole and holy in his presence'*.[1] That's your destiny. He wants you to be happy. Satan has twisted our ideas, confusing holiness with self-righteousness. It's a lie that someone holy is necessarily a miserable, austere, other-worldly presence; who with a severe smile of lofty blessing and a slight frown of disapproval, contrives to make everyone else feel guilty.

There is only one answer to that picture – the name 'Jesus'. In him holiness and happiness were completely entwined. He makes it impossible to envisage holiness without supreme happiness. For any man or woman to be holy is to understand and begin to live out the plan of the Father for them, as someone set apart for God's special purpose. So this holiness is designed to lead us into the ongoing state of supreme happiness.

> *'You are a chosen race, the King's priests, the holy nation, God's own people, chosen to proclaim the wonderful acts of God, who called you out of darkness into his own marvellous light.'*[2]

Absolutely! We are to tell the wonder of him, the one who called us out of darkness into marvellous light, not the complexities of church membership, or doctrine. We are called to witness to Jesus and what he has done for **us**. For he has snapped the chains that shackled us in the prison of our own selfishness. He has freed us from the bondage of keeping rules which can only condemn us. This is why he gave us his own life. We are heirs of God, equipped with the power to live out our individual destiny as he lived his own unique life.

EVERY MOMENT COUNTS

If your life is a once-only opportunity for God to say something original, then you daren't waste it. Every second is a creative moment breathed out by God himself. There is a freedom in knowing that, since every minute matters, **everything** I do is of interest to him. The first realisation of this can be a wild heady experience of undreamt freedom. It is the way Jesus lived.

Jesus was the perfect expression of the law of God. He kept it, as a free man living day by day in his own choices. Because he was **consciously** the son of God uniquely formed by the spirit's activity in Mary's womb, these choices always reflected God's designs. He did what he wanted, and what he wanted always delighted God. His life of freedom is intended for us because we are born of the seed of God as he was.

Perfection is the aim. *'But you are to be perfect even as your Father in heaven is perfect'*, is a direct command with implied promise. This is God's own strategy for transforming ordinary messed-up men and women into the likeness of Christ.

LOVE IS THE KEY

Paul told the church in Galatia that neither keeping the rules nor breaking the rules count for anything, *'but only faith working through love'*.[3] Faith works. It can transform us – but only when it is made effective through love. Love is the heart of our relationship with God. It's the main highway into our hearts for this power. Asked to choose the most important principle in his Jewish Bible, Jesus picked, *'You shall love the Lord your God with all your heart and with all your soul and with all your mind and with all your strength'*[4]; and its companion, *'You shall love your neighbour as yourself'*. He said everything else in the book depends on these principles. As Sir Andrew Lloyd-Webber wrote, 'Love changes everything'.

Being loved by God and loving Him is refreshing. It is a delight to God and a dread to Satan. The world needs more of this sort of Christianity instead of the pale imitation produced by merely keeping the rules. Doctrine, ethics, philosophy and ideals have their place, but they can only produce a colourless copy of the real thing. This is the meaning and purpose of all life and death. We must sometime come to the ultimate human destination – the cross and resurrection of Jesus. Only there can we be set free from the bondage of sin – selfishness, egotism, lustfulness, greed etc. – and released into loving our eternal God.

The command, *'You shall love the Lord your God'* is no longer an instrument of fear exposing our failures. It becomes the key to the power of promise – 'You **shall**'. We hear the unalterable purpose of God: this is how we were meant to be. The command and promise tell us how it will happen. They open to us God's pattern of transformation. John writes *'We love because he first loved us'*.[5] Love starts in God, comes to us, fills us up then flows to other people and back to him. What blocks our access to this love? By far the biggest blockage is guilt, and what it breeds – fear of punishment. We know – it's what we deserve. Yet grace is what God offers instead. Loving generosity is handed to us. We get what we don't deserve – forgiveness and the keys to the family home. Love wins.

We learn to love him with **all the heart**, pouring out on him the fullness of our emotions. All other relationships line up in natural succession. Fierce passion for God like this can reduce all idols – however dear – to ashes in its flame. But it must be expressed. When was the last time you said, 'Oh God, I do love you'?

We love with **all the soul**; the eternal, individual, spiritual essence that makes 'you' who 'you' are. By a determined voluntary attitude of the will, we totally commit ourselves to him. We no longer belong to ourselves. Thus we find the ultimate meaning of who we are, becoming more truly ourselves than we ever were. Human identity is linked unalterably with relationship with God. As the relationship grows, so does our identity.

When God asks for love with **all the mind**, he immediately removes Christianity far from the mystery cults so fashionable today. There are good reasons for loving him, and he expects us to think these through. He expects us to use our minds to see him at work, and understand his ways. We are not called to mindless emotionalism or sentimentality, but to transformation in daily living by the God-centred renewing of our minds.

Loving with all the **strength** is not most obvious in conservative churches. It calls us to use all our physical energy in worship. 'Worship' means giving God what he is worth. How much is that?! Everything, of course!

> 'And so dear brothers and sisters I plead with you to give your bodies to God because of all he has done for you. Let them be a living and holy sacrifice – the kind he will find acceptable. This is truly the way to worship him.'[6]

This means in all of life, but many of us need to accept that our bodies do have a function in worship. We need more vigour in our worship. It's great seeing people free to express love for God with all their strength. A preacher from this country visited a synagogue in New York, when all the men participated in a stately circular dance. He was overwhelmed by the reality of their worship, and later commented, 'I was saddened – there was more glory there under the old covenant than under the new in my church at home'.

FREEDOM OF THE KING'S CHILDREN

We need to relearn the lesson of sonship. Billy Bray, the old Methodist preacher, used to dance on his own in the lanes of Cornwall for sheer amazement and joy that he was 'the King's son'.[7] The Lord came to start a new holy nation of people like him. Living in the present moment with the living God, we really would be free, laughing sons and daughters of the King.

Such a vision is vital if the radical transformation needed by our churches is ever to happen. Without a clear sight of Jesus we will never have the courage to change. Without change, many churches may be by-passed as the Spirit of God moves on. Yet much church life is dominated by fear of change. The instructions of 1 Corinthians 12-14 are totally ignored in the worshipping life of many congregations. No opportunity is given for 'each one' to bring *a hymn, a lesson, a revelation, a tongue or an interpretation'*. [8]

Ignoring that instruction, leaders often quote, *'All things should be done decently and in order'*.[9] Yet there is no need for such sharing to be disorderly, and it adds a new human dimension.

I really believe every individual is called to know God in a way I never can. So every member of Christ can show me something beautiful of him – and I want to see it. We need to pray for the courage of the Spirit of God in church life, and we need to question all those things done simply because 'we've always done it that way'.

Strangely, 'free' churches are often more rigid in pattern than the established ones. Sometimes an unwritten liturgy is harder to change than a written one! Jesus himself changed things which, by familiarity and age, had attained a false sanctity and become spiritual chains that needed to be broken. It is vital that we similarly re-evaluate what we do, on the basis of its effectiveness in communicating Jesus Christ in our culture.

GIFTS OF THE KING'S CHILDREN

One more plea. God has given you a gift, a ministry to the body of Christ. It may be obscure or obvious. Whatever it is, take courage. Seek opportunities to exercise it. Offer to serve. Do it gladly and faithfully – you will find a place of value.

It's not only our worship that needs revolutionary change. For too long we have been happy to bumble along using the same outreach methods as our fathers. We must wake up and smell the coffee! Literally! Café Church creates a sense of community among those invited. Messy Church allows families from toddlers to teenagers to enjoy being in the good news environment. Street Pastors demonstrate the protective care of God for the vulnerable. Healing on the Streets takes the miracle-working love of God into the local community. Food Banks show the caring heart of God for those struggling. 'Christians Against Poverty' offer empowerment to those who feel on the scrapheap. All these are just a few examples of what we can do when we practice Presence evangelism.

'Alpha' has become a world-wide phenomenon with its mix of good food, brief presentation, open discussion and invitation to the Holy Spirit to meet the participants. 'Emmaus' is a similar programme with a more Catholic ethos but still the same mix. There are other similar programmes. These are the two foremost examples of **Process** evangelism.

And there is still a place for a new pattern of outreach using Dance Drama, radical Worship and preaching. **Proclamation evangelism** is still a valid way of presenting the claims of Jesus to a new generation – if it is done with courage and cultural awareness. J.John's "TEN" presentations have reached huge audiences. 'The Message' strategy in Manchester and needy places across the world has had massive impact.

It's time for the siege mentality to go. Everything in our culture indicates an increasing spiritual hunger. We'll need to be radical in our strategies to meet the challenge. But we are the body of Christ. He conquered Hell and Death. What's to be afraid of?

We can learn from the global Church in China, USA, South America, Korea and Africa. Their experiences and our centuries of witness could become a new combine harvester to reap the vast fields which in the words of Jesus are *'white and ripe for harvest'*.

WITNESS OF THE KING'S CHILDREN

Such evangelism must be rooted in costly, loving relationships, inside and between local churches. The gospel is more important than the things which divide us. We dare not play games with the gospel because of our petty politics. We need repentance, **and** bold action. Repentance brings revival, and that's the context in which the message of the kingdom is truly effective. Jesus had compassion on the multitudes. Let's join him in that compassion, by giving ourselves to prayer that hundreds of thousands of people will be brought into the kingdom of God. It will take costly personal witness, authentic gospel presentation, and commitment to effective social action.

Hudson Taylor, the hero of China, once wrote, 'Too often we attempt to work for God to the limit of our incompetence. We should work to the limits of his omnipotence'.

When it comes to our personal witness, as J.John says we are too often 'like Arctic Rivers – frozen at the mouth!' What will convince people that we have eternal life? Being irrepressibly full of joy and love – even in pain and distress, authenticates our witness. Often faced with the opportunity to speak for Christ, we mumble about going to church. Great – if your church is vibrant, exciting and relevant with a great online presence. What about mentioning Jesus himself as your closest friend and guide? Presented right, he is fascinating. You could become known not just as religious but as a follower of Jesus! Why not try this? Get to work early. Walk round the workplace praying. Claim the ground for God and bless everyone who works there. You could be surprised! As you liberate him to reign in the place where you work he will set you free.

HOLINESS OF THE KING'S CHILDREN

God has called you to live for him in your unique situation: butcher, bank clerk, P.A., waste disposal operative, computer programmer, warehouseman, doctor, road sweeper, consultant, nurse, home carer, family management operative – (mum/ dad!), retiree, student or tycoon. Yield that to him so he becomes your unseen 'boss'. Nobody else can live for Christ in the job you do. That's your privilege and pain. It's different from anyone else's. That makes is special in God's kingdom – HOLY! Commit it to Jesus so it becomes an adventure.

Holiness is not the absence of badness, but the positive presence of the life of Jesus. Your destiny is to live with him so that every moment becomes holy, lit up with heavenly meaning. You see, Jesus has set his name on you. His reputation is riding on you. He chose to continue his incarnation in you. But there are risks. Allow the Lord to reign and he triumphs in you over the world, the flesh and the devil. You triumph – Satan cringes. However, refuse to live in obedience to him, and disaster is near. You crash and burn. The Lord's name is disgraced – and Satan and his angels rejoice in triumph.

No wonder C. T. Studd wrote:

> *'Let us not rust out. Let us not glide through the world and then slip quietly out without ever having blown the trumpet loud and long for our blessed redeemer. At the very least let us see to it that the Devil holds a thanksgiving service in hell when he gets the news of our departure from the field of battle!'*

Totally YES!

Holiness is godliness with guts. God has made it available to all his people. So why do we fall so far short?

Dedicated, committed, consecrated; then re-dedicated, re-committed and re-consecrated; filled with the Spirit, refilled. What stops us from possessing the land? What prevents us from moving in the reality of the destiny formed for 'me' from eternity? It is to our greatest problem that we turn in the next chapter.

But first... remember Peter and John, skilled working men unafraid to confront the highest in the land? They were gutsy, gritty characters – one of whom had betrayed Jesus. Yet they demonstrated courage in living which had so obviously come from their encounter with Christ. When Peter and Jesus met after the resurrection, Jesus had no reproach for Peter who had denied him with curses. He had a question, three times. *'Do you love me?'* Each time Peter said, *'Yes, I do.'* Each time Jesus said *'I gave you the task of caring for those I love; will you take it up again and not turn back?'* Peter said, *'I will'.* That's what makes a real man or woman. The willingness to face failure – then look their God full in the face, accept forgiveness, and commit themselves again to the task that is their destiny.

Never give up.

> **'Lord,**
> **I long to be a true disciple,**
> **Forgive me for the times**
> **I draw back in fear.**
> **May the love I feel for you**
> **grow to fill my whole being.**
> **Give me the courage**
> **to let go of all idols,**
> **And the guts to follow**
> **when it's really tough.**
> **By faith I abandon myself**
> **to the flow of your love.**
> **Amen.'**

CHAPTER 7

FACING INTO THE SUN

'LET'S GO AT ONCE AND TELL...'

Evening at last. All day the sun had beaten down from a cloudless sky. Now the sun was sinking. As the rocks lost their heat it would be cold. The four men in the shanty nestled close to the city wall pulled ragged coats about them. They had not always been beggars. One had been a prosperous businessman, another a craftsman in metals, the others labourers. Now they were united in two ghastly fellowships, they were lepers, and they were starving.

Wordlessly they gathered their meagre possessions, and tried to make their tattered clothing more presentable. Talk was superfluous. They had done all that during the day, and had reached an agreement. Tonight they were going to die – or eat for the first time in days, and live. People said, 'Poor things, they'd be better off dead'. But they wanted to live, so much so, that this evening they were going to walk across enemy lines and into the Syrian camp. The walls of the besieged city shone in the dying rays of the evening sun as the men took their last look. Inside, Famine ruled. Haggard, starving women had killed and eaten new-born babies, men bargained five pieces of silver for half a litre of dove's dung – to eat!

It was time to leave.

Approaching the Syrian camp they were too nervous to notice the quiet. This time in the evening should have been full of the noises of army camp life: evening trumpets calling, wood being cut for the fires, cooking pots bubbling, sentries on guard duty exchanging good-humoured insults prior to the changing of duties.

They reached the forward lines only to find an abandoned sentry post. In the camp itself there was nobody to be seen. Tethered horses whinnied in greeting, but there was no trace of the besieging army. Everywhere were signs of panic, equipment abandoned, uniforms scattered, and food – lots of lovely food.

Now reality hit. The Syrians had gone, without taking the food. They gorged until the hunger of months was satisfied with rich food and wine. Then they began to loot the camp of valuables which they put in a secret stash.

Then one of them remembered his family in the city! Where men and women waited for death to come on slow feet.

> 'We shouldn't be doing this! We have good news and we shouldn't keep it to ourselves. If we wait until morning to tell it, we are sure to be punished. Let's go at once and tell…'

Precisely. Absolutely right!

Our world is besieged by Hell's powers, spiritually starving, haunted by guilt and desperately lonely. We stuff ourselves full of the good news but we don't pass it on.

OUR GREAT GOSPEL

Twice, Mark records Jesus commending sacrifice *'for my sake and for the Good News',*[2] giving the **good news** the same priority as himself. Both Mark and Luke record Jesus linking loyalty to himself with loyalty to his words: *'if anyone is ashamed of me and my words...'*[3]

What is this gospel that is so important to Jesus? First, it is the good news of the kingdom of **Heaven**. It is a royal proclamation announcing the rule of heaven's king here on earth. Believing it, humans can leave the kingdom of darkness which overshadows this world, and become citizens of heaven while still living here on earth. It's marvellous news. Heaven is near. Long before death I can begin to live in heaven's reality.

Second, it is the kingdom of **God**: the wonderful news that God's authority is re-established on our rebellious earth. Sin, death, misery and pain **will** one day be defeated. We can escape the fearful authority of Satan and enter our Father's kingdom. His Son is proclaimed as King in majesty for ever, whose kingly power is founded on love, guaranteed by his battle-scarred body.

So the prime aim of the gospel is not just the forgiveness of sins, but the reign of God in Christ. The objective of the gospel is the life of Christ – each Christian man and woman living as Jesus would have lived in their time with their name. The gospel sets us free to shout to a world in confusion, 'You can be what you are meant to be; your true destiny awaits you'. Proclaiming that is **our** true destiny!

OUR STRANGE SILENCE

So many of our blessings are conditional on our courage in witnessing, our commitment to the gospel. The promise *"I am with you always"* is made in the context of *'go and make disciples of all nations'*.[4] Our assurance of salvation depends on our speaking out the Lordship of Jesus.[5] Paul encouraged Timothy to pray for the authorities so we could have a *'quiet and peaceable life'*[6] because this was good for the spread of the gospel. If we are to enjoy the riches of our destiny we must become 'good-newsers'.

Comments on religious matters thrown out apparently carelessly, in the workplace, at the bar or in the coffee shop, are often made as challenges. We need to learn the art of responding creatively in these moments. We are the message. We must **be** the gospel. Through us the vibrant abundance of the life of God bursts into the world. You and I are irreplaceable parts of the Message.

GOD'S GROWING GOVERNMENT

It was not only the gospel that Jesus placed on a par with himself. In Luke 18:29 he promised untold blessings to those who left property, relationships and family ties for the sake of the Kingdom – just as he had asked them to leave these things for His own sake. He required a love for the kingdom so high that by comparison we might be accused of 'hating' parents, wife, brothers and sisters and our own life. No other considerations matter. God's will alone counts, and it is to the onward march of that will that you have pledged yourself in joining his kingdom.

Sometimes in our fear we misinterpret his purpose. When we have lived under repression or brutal domination, we may retreat from him. 'God's government' can feel like the threat of an obsessional control freak.

The opposite is true. Paul wrote in the letter to the church in Galatia, *'Christ has set us free to live a **free life'**.*[7] God is free. We are his children. He made us to be free like he is. That's why Paul wrote to his *'son in the gospel'* Timothy, *'God did not give us a spirit that makes us afraid, but a spirit of power and love and **self**-control'.*[8]

Freedom is the name of God's game. He wants to set us free from everything we hold – or that holds us – so that we can create, climb, cooperate and play like the Holy Trinity. He is looking forward to seeing what the new creation will produce from us. He's like any proud parent: "See that – my girl did that, my boy made that."

IN LOVE HE SETS US FREE.

C. S. Lewis once called God 'the Celestial Interferer' because God insists on disrupting everything in us that runs counter to his purpose, or stands higher in our affections than Him. He does this out of his love for us. As his government increases, so does his peace. Continually learning his will in day by day encounter, we grow in the resurrection life of Christ.

And the onward march of his kingdom continues.

In us the God of heaven confronts the god of this world. Our King is supremely worthy of his authority – for he won it by winning the love of our hearts. Living under the authority of 'another King, Jesus' we are the frontier between heaven and earth. The plan is that by prayer and Spirit-inspired action we should extend that frontier to encompass others. Satan doesn't like that idea! Not surprisingly he tries to convince us that the job is too hard.

WEAKNESS WITHIN

If he succeeds then we no longer live with an eager offensive spirit scenting victory everywhere we go. Apathetically we retreat into the church subculture, where we may be soothed by comforting religious experience. This is **not** the time to take things easy. We are part of the mighty invasion force of the King of kings. The great missionary explorer David Livingstone said, 'I will place no value on anything I may have or possess except as it shall further the kingdom of God'. So let's be bold and give this world a glimpse of the future Kingdom through an ongoing daily experience of Jesus changing us.

Anything less is not 'life' at all but a sub-life. It's terrifyingly possible for the **words** 'a personal relationship with Jesus Christ' to become a substitute for **living** that relationship. How do we escape? Daily repentance helps. *'Repent, for the kingdom of Heaven is near,'* [9] Jesus said. The kingdom is always near to a repentant person. A life open to the Heavenly Kingdom is exciting, an adventure because it involves walking in a growing awareness of God.

THE TRANSFORMING VISION

At the centre of the kingdom and the heart of the gospel is Jesus himself. We're not dealing primarily with a system of doctrine, philosophy, ethics, morals or ideals. Christianity is Jesus himself – a man to be loved, a friend to walk with, a master to be served, a King to be obeyed, and a saviour to be received. God supreme, in all things to be worshipped. A wrong vision of Jesus will be disastrous, inevitably producing a to a distorted version of Christian living. We must have a clear vision of him – the best and bravest human ever. To see him clearly by the Spirit is to be captivated. This is the love we've searched for. This is the real thing.

Like all love affairs it will transform the lover – into the likeness of the beloved.

It is the nature of lovers to gaze at each other for hours. In fact it's often hard to get them to do anything else! Gazing on Christ with our inward eyes is the key to the art of contemplation – the Holy Spirit in me meeting the Jesus of scripture. A vision of him is always transforming. So the man or woman who has seen *'the light of the knowledge of the glory of God in the face of Jesus Christ'* [10] will find that glory settling in them, with potential to raise them from one level of glory to another.

This is the basic principle of Christian transformation: a vision of Jesus so real that it changes us by penetrating to the roots of our personality. Before this can happen we must believe it is possible. This may be the greatest barrier to progress.

THE TYRANNY OF FEELINGS

The most fundamental problem of all humans facing their holy maker is the tyranny of feelings. When Satan seduced humanity away from intimate relationship with the eternal God, he polluted our humanity so thoroughly, it was no longer possible for us to know God as we were designed to – perfectly and thoroughly flooding through every sense we possess.

He seeded a vague feeling of doubt in Eve about what God had said. He then reinforced it by telling her God's motives were selfish. She clearly knew by past experience that God was good. But slowly, carefully, Satan constructed a false picture of God and her own feelings.

He then appealed to her appetite, love of beauty and intellectual vanity. In response, she elevated the doubt, and the aroused desires to mastery over herself. Deciding to follow her lead, Adam ratified her decision to trust present feelings over the promise of God, adding the twist of his own feelings for her. From that instant man and woman were subjected to a new inner tyranny – the ever-present need to fulfil the desire of the moment. No one ever can satisfy every desire immediately, so disappointment became the background to life. Earthly kings, megastars and tyrants who were nearest to being able to satisfy every desire, experienced the greatest disillusion and emptiness. Disappointment, inner sadness and cynicism became all too common to the human race.

THE LYING VISION

Satan plays on our expectations, then dashes the hopes aroused. He constantly plays on the profound doubt of promised good sitting deep in all of us. Our enemy has painstakingly constructed in us a gaping void of mistrust. He wants us to feel that, if God is real, he is mean, selfish, arbitrary and cynical. He rarely denies God's power to help us. He presents someone playing games with human beings, lips curled in amusement as he watches them struggle; whose loving is selfish manipulation for his own ends.

This picture finds ready acceptance in us. Our own behaviour is too often like this – we know we deserve this sort of God. But the Bible cuts right across it.

> *'Give thanks to the Lord, for he is good! His steadfast love endures forever.'*[11]

Repeatedly God's sheer goodness and unselfish loving is affirmed. Often, those who say that they have intellectual problems believing in a good God are controlled by the subjective reaction that **prefers** a wicked or amoral God. That lays on them no moral imperative to change.

God has spoken through his creation, his written Word and the eternal Word himself. The consistent message is, 'The Father himself loves you'. With total confidence I can promise, 'God actually loves you, and He always has. He has only one plan – that is for you to be changed by the power of the Holy Spirit to be like Jesus Christ, so that people who meet you will be able to say, "Now I know what Jesus is like. I've met him"'.

BREAK THE BONDAGE

That's his destiny for you, and nothing can stop it but your unbelief. You can decide to accept that God actually means this for **you**. He does – so now, once for all, break free! Smash the bondage of mere feelings! Stand, a free woman or man, before the living God and commit yourself to the objective facts of his holy goodness, his selfless loving and the absolute reality of his revelation in Christ. Ignore your negativity, and the judgement of your guilty heart that declares you are not good enough to merit God's goodness. It's all lies because the emphasis is wrong. It's God the Father who is good enough to love you, accept you, be proud of you and call you His child. Don't run from this. God is GOOD and good to you.

You must give him the clear, coolly calculated conviction of your mind, and commit yourself to it – 'Jesus is **truth**. Jesus is God, God is love. These things I believe, **irrespective of my feelings of guilt, fear and unworthiness.'** Once you settle yourself on that, a new reality begins. Then you must give him the same calculated coolness in a total commitment of the will.

'Jesus Christ, you are Lord and God. You died for me because of your great love for me. My feelings are unreliable. I want you to know that irrespective of my feelings, I love you. More important, Father, I accept by love your love for me, your approval of me and your identification of me as your child. Even if only ten per cent of me wants you, I commit myself by voluntary act of the will to that ten per cent. I want you more than my own comfort. I love you now and will love you always. I can tell you this because I believe you are bigger than my fears and failures. You love me because you are Love with a capital "L!". You are my real Father. In you I have come home. Thank you.'

Pray like this, and you are taking the first steps in the process of bringing your feelings into submission to Christ. You are taking those turbulent, rebellious, things inside you, into **your** service, by subjecting them to your King. Clearly, it's not simply a matter of saying words like those above, but of involving **yourself** in such spoken commitments. Your feelings must become your servants. Let them **follow** facts and they will run obediently along behind them, releasing life, joy and spontaneity. This pulsating, invigorating flow is not the object of our believing, but it will be the outcome. So take charge! Remember David's orders to himself,

'*Praise the Lord,* ***O my soul, all my inmost being,*** *praise his holy name.*'[12]

This doesn't mean we should be dishonest. Honesty is vital. Give the way you feel to God. Faith only demands this should no longer be dominant. Tell the Father your heart is breaking, disaster threatens on every hand, and you can't go on; while with tears streaming down your face you are also saying, 'But I trust you and praise you, for you **are** great and you **love me**'. That's real biblical love: total dedication of the whole person to the good of another. It hurts! Of course.

> 'Those who belong to Jesus Christ have nailed the passions and desires of their sinful nature to his cross, and crucified them there.'[13]

Paul called this dying with Christ. Drastic? Maybe – but it is better than living without him.

Moses discovered that.

THE FIERY VISION

A bush suddenly burst into flame. Out in the wild semi-desert near Mount Sinai flash fires were not unusual in the blazing heat of midday. Moses continued, the flock following as he looked for good grass. It caught his eye again, still burning, which was odd. Normally they lasted only a few moments. But this one showed no sign of dying down. Then he noticed something really strange. In spite of the white intensity of the fire the bush was not burning.

Curiosity drew him nearer. There was no ash and no smoke rising. A tingling sense of something strange ran through him. Even the sheep seemed hushed.

'Moses, Moses!' The voice was rich and full. It came from the heart of the flame.

'Here I am.'

Again the voice, glad, untamed and holy:

> *'Don't come any closer. Remove your sandals from your feet. You're standing on holy ground. I am the God of your father, the God of Abraham, the God of Isaac, the God of Jacob.'*[14]

Fear ran through Moses. Now he knew why the flame had seared not only his eyes but his whole being. A swift movement brought his hood down low over his face – he was afraid to look any longer at the brightness.

That day Moses entered the service of the living God. Reluctant, afraid, unable to believe that he was actually chosen by the almighty, he entered upon his destiny. A less auspicious start could hardly be imagined. Yet Moses would become a man of epic proportions, a mighty deliverer and great leader.

The vision at the bush became his driving passion. He'd seen something at Sinai that he loved. Years later it drew him back with one aim. Trembling with fear he walked up the mountain to see God face to face. He finally came down transformed.

His face shone. The radiation of God's holiness had poured into him: living purity, eternal truth and pure love had taken him to the limit of human capacity. God had answered his prayer. After his death, the historian wrote,

> 'No prophet has risen since in Israel like Moses, whom God knew face-to-face.'[15]

In the New Covenant, God went further – he took the light that shone on Sinai and placed it in us. Just watch this: Paul writes, *'God has shone in our hearts to give the light of the knowledge of the glory of God in the face of Jesus Christ'.*[16] The Father has placed that **inside** us – now. Unbelievable! But true.

THE FEAR WE MUST CONFRONT

So why don't we believe it? Because we hold on to the idea that we'll only get what we deserve. God's goodness to the undeserving contradicts our expectations – surely He can't forgive **us**? So we opt to believe Satan's lie that whispers our failures, our secret sins and guilt. We hold these in front of the God we have created from our fears – the false God we feel we deserve who will judge us as we expect. It's easier to believe in this idol than to take the step of faith – to believe in the God who is Love who holds out to us unlimited grace. It takes courage beyond the normal to commit to that outstretched hand. But it's the only way we can be changed.

The problem is his holiness, his total purity and love. Confronted with a love sacrificially committed to our ultimate good, and the limitless happiness that only comes from holiness, we are bound to feel discomfort. His holiness and perfection confront my imperfection. This hurts, so we fear to come near to God. Only one thing to do then – resolve to come closer!

As we draw near to Him we must open up to the pain of his probing love as it digs deeper into 'me', determined to cut out every last tendril of sin.

THE PAIN WE MUST ACCEPT

So if we're to live in the power of the Spirit, we must be prepared to live with pain when confronted with the holiness of God. This is a happy pain. It becomes a gateway to the joy of victory.

Few things in the human body provide a better picture of sin than cancer. Relating sin to cancer, new birth is the moment when the main growth is cut out. Part of holiness is the lifelong commitment to let God cut deeper and deeper, following the winding roots of sinfulness into the foundations of our conscious and subconscious being. The pathways cleared are opened to the Holy Spirit – the river of life, given to us without limit. He draws us in two directions: into the needy world and into our loving Father's heart. So the world's torment will meet with God's redeeming love. There will be a cross in us, in me.

Sadly today such phrases as 'I die daily' and 'I have been crucified with Christ', have become poetic exaggeration, rather than literal description of a real experience. Worse, they have become the kind of language one expects of a 'Premier League' Christian like St Paul – but not the present experience of an 'ordinary' Christian still in the 'Sunday League', or 'Little League'.

This is dangerous, because it enables us to live consistently below New Testament standards – without feeling guilty about it. 'No one expects the same standard of football from non-league clubs as from Premier League giants. It's nice to be idealistic, but we've got to be real.' Worse still, this can affect our view of Jesus. 'All right for him to talk about loving God with all the heart, soul, mind and strength: after all, he was perfect. Nobody else is…'

THE GOAL WE SHOULD AIM AT

We easily forget his command, 'Be perfect'. But we have the promise of power, not only the map but also the fuel. The Spirit of God really can take an ordinary man or woman right into the purifying furnace of the heart of God. He'll do it for us if we will let him – and right there is the heart of the issue. Will we let him? It's about trust. Intimacy. Will I trust his love and give him access?

God doesn't reveal his holiness to condemn us, but to transform us from the inside by a constant process of cleansing, healing and refilling. All he needs from us is a moment by moment response of trust and repentance agreeing that God is right and we are wrong. Sin begins to die as we continually expose it to the radiation of God's holiness. We are usually surprised by this encounter. Instead of condemnation and rejection, we get challenge, encouragement and acceptance.

Many years ago after a particularly stupid incident, a really good friend asked me a tough question, "Eric, with all the gifts God has given you, why do you do these stupid things?" Looking at the floor I could only reply, "I don't know." But I kept on asking myself, "Why am I the way I am?" I began to see that wounds way back in the past had left me very vulnerable to certain temptations. When I asked God to touch those areas, the Holy Spirit came. Swift as an arrow, gentle as a dove, clever as a bloodhound, he came seeking and healing those places. Like the Good Samaritan with the mugging victim, he poured into my wounds oil to soothe and heal, wine to cleanse. His gentleness woos us rather than threatens.

As we live before him, repentant and open; we live in the now with God who is always in the 'now'. We begin sharing that state of eternity known as everlasting life. At last!

We start to do the will of the Father naturally, because we want to. This is the service that is perfect freedom: the joyous liberation of finally finding out what we truly want. The great reformer, Luther, wrote 'Love God and do as you like.'

Practical pointers:

- Practise positive prayer. No reciting your troubles. No long 'shopping lists'. Tell God how good, loving and great he is. **Practise** telling him you love him.

- Look for him in other Christians. Find someone who **knows** God better than you do. Commit yourself to them. Learn what they've learnt. God's transforming power through their experiences will encourage you.

- Look for the **present tense** in Scripture. Romans Chapter 4 describes God's action in history. Chapter 5 moves into present experience The present tense emphasised in Chapter 8. Enter that reality – God is always present tense.

This prayer may help you.

'Lord
you are great,
the Maker of all things.
Forgive me that I so often run from you,
when I long to move towards you.
Take charge of my emotions.
Reign over them, that they may
become a pathway for your Spirit.
Make me holy, that I may be truly happy.
Through Jesus, who radiates gladness.
Amen.'

CHAPTER 8
FACTS ARE BETTER THAN DREAMS

'Although impatient for the morning I slept soundly and had no need of cheering dreams. Facts are better than dreams.'[1]

THE BIBLE - TRUTH IS NOT BORING

The Bible. The most important and fascinating book the world has ever seen. Not so much a book – more a library of life, encompassing a bigger vision of each person and their place in the whole creation than anyone ever dreamed of. Starting with the making of the universe it ends with its destruction and remaking. Not just earthbound, it rises even above the galaxies and places humanity in a cosmic context.

The first historical books present a picture of human lives intertwined with great events on a scale that dwarfs *'The Lord of the Rings'* or *'War and Peace'*. The cast list includes heroes, villains, kings, shepherds, farmers, murderers, thieves, rapists, saints, prophets, priests, lovers and a talking donkey. Later the history weaves its pattern around two kingdoms; one with its long dynasty from a single family, and the other featuring a series of bloody coups that make our own history look positively anaemic. Successive invasions by ruthless armies of conquest from empires to the east and south, end in the collapse first of one and finally the other kingdom. Then follows the agony of a nation in chains as the Jewish people are dragged into exile.

But they have endured – through millennia. In the Classic movie, 'Chariots of Fire', Sir John Gielgud, playing the

Master of Trinity College, watches Ben Cross playing Harold Abrahams complete the 'College Dash'. It's never been done before.

"Well, it's been done by a Caius College man – the first man in seven centuries. Perhaps they really are God's chosen people after all?"

And they are. With all their struggles and failures through the centuries, God has never stopped loving the Jews. Jesus is the crowning glory of this amazingly enduring and talented people. The beginning of their epic saga is the theme of the Old Testament.

Through it all is the never-ending love of God to whom they pledged themselves in covenant relationship, only to break the covenant repeatedly. His loyal love for the nations of Israel and Judah is a song of heartbreak. Repeated rebellion makes it necessary for the loving Father of Israel to act – discipline is the pain-filled obligation of parental love. While all this is happening fascinating characters emerge for a moment, then disappear again: Benaiah went down into a pit on a snowy day. Why? The Bible doesn't say – but while he was there he killed a lion; Jael gave a bottle of milk to the wicked tyrant Sisera and then banged a tent peg into his head while he slept!

Boring? How could anyone say it was boring? Vast in its scope and often gruesome in its factual depiction of human wickedness, it may be difficult in places but boring – never! And it's all true.

THE BIBLE –
REAL RELATIONSHIPS WITH A REAL GOD

It really happened. It is a record of the actions of the living God in relationship with human beings, the story of his long battle with Satan to prevent him from dragging the billions on earth into hellish misery and emptiness. God has acted in human history and people have either joined him or fought him.

From those who committed themselves to him came poetry and drama – often sublime in their imagery, a unique collection of personal experiences. They plumb the depths of human misery, rising through great happiness to the very edges of God-given bliss. Then books of history, prophecy and ancient lament known as the prophets. Full of passion and burning calls for revolutionary change in society, these books have stimulated, excited and scared the people of God through centuries. They are still frighteningly relevant.

The prophets' promise that God will come to his people is thrillingly fulfilled in the Gospels by the coming of Jesus and the gift of the Holy Spirit. That invasion of life and joy launches the Church. Within this growing community letters are exchanged that still today sparkle with bubbling life. The book is crowned by an amazing piece of literature called Revelation. Often discredited by the idiocy of Christianity's fringe 'loonies' it is the most marvellous epic romance in the world. The bride-to-be is held in terrible captivity by a wicked dragon for years of torment. Tortured, wounded, often appearing near to death, she holds on in hope, believing that one day her prince will come. Then he does come, riding a white horse – a conqueror who destroys the dragon, rescues her and carries her off to live with him for ever. Never were the words truer, 'And they all lived happily ever after'.

That part is yet to be. But, have no doubt, it will happen, for the Bible is utterly reliable. Facts, facts, facts from beginning to end.

THE BIBLE – RELIABLE TRUTH

'Facts are better than dreams.' When Churchill wrote that, he was speaking as a warrior faced with the task of winning a war. Whatever you personally may think of him, his assessment of the position was correct. In such a situation a man or woman needs facts. Solid facts. And the Bible is solidly factual, stubbornly reliable, historically, archaeologically and scientifically. It is also reassuringly human.

Some years ago I did a survey of people's attitude to Jesus and the church for Local Radio. I asked first, 'What do you think of the Church?' Some of the replies were unprintable, others typical.

One rather generously proportioned, breathy lady in her fifties beamed at the question. Her wide-brimmed hat and impeccable clothes oozed prosperity.

'The church? Wonderful, wonderful.'

'Thank you. Would you mind telling me how often you go to church?'

'Oh, every week. Would never miss it.'

'I see. What do you think of Jesus?' Her smile vanished.

'Jesus? Oh, nothing at all. He's nothing to do with it. Some form of Higher Thought. That's what matters.'

She certainly would not have approved of the Bible's earthiness about King Saul entering a cave to relieve himself, or the promise of the Rabshakeh to the besieged population of Samaria that they would be reduced to eating their own dung. Such things hardly come under the heading of Higher Thought!

But the Bible is embarrassingly frank even about basic biology. It is completely honest about our humanity and our fallenness. From beginning to end it is inspired by the Spirit of God who can never lie. The writers can't ever put a gloss on any character, or dress him up! The characters are there 'warts and all'. It never tries to 'improve on' or embroider events. It is historically reliable because the Spirit of God wouldn't allow anyone to alter history.

The New Testament is already recognised by many historians as being the most reliable historical document of its time; and the Old Testament, once so besieged by critics, is steadily being vindicated as archaeology produces more and more evidence to confirm its record. It's rather fun to see critics retreat in confusion!

THE BIBLE - INCONVENIENT TRUTH

Of course, some philosophers and theologians still attack the biblical story but more on philosophical grounds. Since much modern philosophy is directed largely by subjective preference, not facts, there is no refuting such views. One suspects they prefer it that way. [2]

Sometimes Christians are accused of wishful thinking when it comes to the authority of the Bible. In my case I must confess this is true. I have often wished that it were **not** authoritative; for moral, or rather immoral reasons! But I'm glad this book boldly continues to denounce my behaviour, until I return in honest confession to Jesus Christ and there find forgiveness, and power to live right.

The spirit of our age is very proud. It is part of our cultural conditioning that we are more technologically advanced than people of previous centuries, and therefore the further back in history, the more primitive people were. Breathtaking! Try telling that to Pythagoras!

Some say that while they can accept Jesus as real and even the son of God, they cannot accept the Old Testament. When asked why Jesus and the apostles under the influence of the Holy Spirit believed it to be true, they say they were 'prisoners of their culture'. This is such nonsense. If ever a man was free – really free – Jesus was that man; never was a man less a prisoner of his time or his environment. He was intellectually, emotionally and spiritually free under the Father's guidance. We are the real prisoners when we cannot break free of the arrogance of our age and accept the timelessness of truth. The Bible is true.

THE BIBLE – PERMANENT TRUTH

The spirit of our time also seeks to destroy any idea of the permanence of truth, and replace it by a disposable throwaway faith which happens to be 'true for me at this moment'. The poet Steve Turner wrote a brilliantly biting parody of this, called 'Creed'. Part of it goes:

> 'I believe that each man must find
> the truth that is right for him.
> Reality will adapt accordingly.
> The universe will readjust.
> History will alter.
> I believe that there is no absolute truth,
> excepting the truth that there is no absolute truth.'[3]

Some Christian people hold to a religious version of that. A university chaplain once told me 'There is no minimum of faith necessary to be a Christian'. Such people are well-meaning robbers of the faith. They destroy the foundations of Christian belief – all in the name of a God of love, whose actual character and person become vaguer and emptier the longer one looks. They think they are helping, but in fact they rob people of God-given assurance.

Their church becomes a dream factory dominated by 'spirituality' closer to paganism than the spirit of Christ.

Elitism is inevitable. The church of Jesus Christ who valued all he met becomes the dominion of the 'naturally spiritual', the ones with secret knowledge.

Thank God for the facts! Everybody – naturally 'religious' or not – can trust the written Word of God, and so meet Jesus, eternally the Word of God in person. That's the whole purpose of the Bible. God-breathed, it calls us to know the Father-Maker, providing all the information we need, pointing infallibly to him.

But knowing the Bible is not the same as knowing God. For some the written Word becomes more important than Jesus – the Word himself. The map has become more important than the destination. This is a terrible perversion. It's idolatry, or even – 'bibliolatry'. Because of its nature, this temptation usually afflicts religious people of orthodox, Protestant, belief.

THE BIBLE – THE WAY TO THE WAY

The Pharisees were orthodox. They upheld a high view of their Jewish Bible as inspired by God and infallible. Yet Jesus said to them,

> 'You search the scriptures, because you believe they give you eternal life. But the scriptures point to me. Yet you refuse to come to me so that I can give you this eternal life.'[4]

The scriptures are meant to lead us to him. When they don't, it's tragic. To read the written words of God and not through them hear his voice inwardly, is a terrible denial of their purpose.

For the quest to know God as no one else ever did begins here – before the open pages of the Bible. Through this rich and varied book, God can speak to you as he never quite spoke to anyone. His unique revelation of himself to you starts here. It's the only sure way into his heart – for in these pages he has bared his heart:

> *'My anguish, my anguish! I writhe in pain! Oh, the walls of my heart! My heart is beating wildly; I cannot keep silent; for I hear the sound of the trumpet, the alarm of war.'*[5]

That is the agony of a loving Father watching his rebellious children plunging headlong into the misery of war. God's purpose is to lead you through the gateway of those words into him. However, you must recognise that only God can reveal the truth about himself. Therefore if you are to know him – even through the Bible – you must let the Spirit of God lead you, otherwise it will be a dead book to you.

THE BIBLE – THE WORD OF THE WORD

Earlier, we talked about Jesus' title, the Word of God. The Bible is also called the Word of God – that is the written revelation of God – just as Jesus is the definitive human revelation of

God. The written Word comes to us by the Holy Spirit, from the eternal Word. So it is the word of the Word of God. Jesus Christ, the eternal Word, is revealed in every part of the Bible. He waits to meet you in different ways on every page.

Here we plunge back into the mainstream of our theme. You are unique, different from anyone else ever born. When God spoke out the word that became you, he said something he'd never said before – and will never say again. Therefore when the Bible's message meets you, God reveals a fresh facet of Himself. God has things to say to **you** through the Bible that no-one else could ever hear in the same way.

The living God, limitless in personality and creation, has so much to say and only eternity in which to say it! We can all know the broad outlines of his character – the soaring mountain peaks of his holiness, the warm spice-scented valleys of his love, the ocean-dark depths of his humility. But the intimate aspects of him as Father and lover we can discover only as we know him, one to one. The holy ground on which we stand as we do this is the infallible rock of God's book.

APPROACH IT WITH THOUGHT

We are not to be superstitious about the Bible. We are to use our brains to try to understand and apply its teaching. *'Study… to be a workman who has no cause to be ashamed, correctly analysing and accurately dividing the word of truth.'*[6] But we are never to elevate reason above the Bible. If something is true but beyond our understanding, that doesn't mean it's untrue! It simply means that we don't yet have the insight to grasp it.

Spiritual perception grows within us as we are exposed to the voice of God. The surest way to hear that voice is through reading the Bible, while remaining open to the Holy Spirit. The Bible is spiritual food. Therefore we should read it with expectation of receiving a revelation of Jesus.

Remember, brilliant theologians can study the Bible for years and never see Jesus as who he is – the eternal God in flesh. Whoever we are, leaders or not, we should read the Bible not primarily to formulate doctrines, but to know God in Christ. **Our** theology should spring out of faith and reason meeting revelation.

As has often been said, 'Jesus is perfect theology'. That's profoundly true. So Jesus Christ **is** the key to the Bible. Once we have received him as King and friend, he begins to unlock the mysteries of the book. So we can expect him to show us something every day **provided we ask him**, in faith.

APPROACH IT WITH PRAYER

'Jesus Christ, you are the Word, the message of the Father God. I want to know you. As I read this book give me your Spirit and make yourself real to me, As I get to know you, make the Father real to me too, so that I will know him and begin to live like his child.'

Approach the Bible with that kind of prayer and I promise you God will speak to you, though not always in the same way. As I've said, it is spiritual food. But food comes in many forms.

Sometimes I take my wife out to a restaurant for a beautifully prepared and presented meal. We really enjoy these occasions, but there are times when a poached egg on toast or fish pie with mashed potatoes and peas can taste like food of the gods. And what about Indian and Chinese food – not to mention American favourites? Or great thick chocolate éclairs oozing dairy cream; crusty wholemeal rolls filled with fresh lettuce, tomatoes, mayo and a slice of ham; a bowl of porridge, or simply a piece of crusty bread torn from a fresh loaf with a bowl of soup; all of it is food. Some foods are more exciting than others – they all have their place in a healthy diet. Sometimes Bible reading is stodgy like a bowl of porridge, but it is food and is building you up though you may not know it. For the living Christ is in it all. And that's why every Christian should read the whole Bible. The whole Bible? What?! Yes, but not all at once. We'll look at how later.

An old Anglican Prayer Book calls the communion service 'a holy mystery', saying Jesus is present in the bread and wine in a spiritual and heavenly way. Likewise, Jesus is present in the Bible – mystically, spiritually, truly there. It is an book made of ordinary paper and ink. But when you open its pages to seek him, he pours out the power of his presence to meet you and fill you. The reality expressed in words on paper is conveyed by the Holy Spirit into you. You are feeding on the living God. And just as Jesus promised, this feeding on him – this recognition that here is the one whose body was broken for *me*, whose blood was spilt for *me* – brings life! For the life of God is in his love letter to you. When your ears are spiritually open you hear him saying, 'I love you.'

Set in this kind of relationship, God guiding you is no longer the 'hit and miss' business it can seem to be. The key is first knowing the sound of God's voice. Reading the Bible attunes your spiritual ear, so you recognise his call.

APPROACH IT WITH SENSE

'OK so it's great. I tried to read the whole Bible and got stuck halfway through Exodus. All those curtains, rods and rings, fine-twined linen, badger skins and tent pegs! I couldn't keep going. It was so boring! What does all that have to do with Jesus?' The answer is, 'Right now, not very much. To make that connection, you have to know a lot more about Jesus.'

Let's get practical. Many people know they ought to read their Bibles but never do it. How do I begin? First, for most people beginning at Genesis and reading through to Revelation is just not possible. Jesus is the key to the whole book, so a basic reading knowledge of the New Testament, will help to light up the Old Testament. There are many ways to study the Bible, but the most important is simply to read it; because reading is the basis for all other methods of study.

So how do you start?

If you've had trouble with Bible reading before, you would probably find it helpful to buy a new one, one of the modern versions. Go online, or to a good bookshop. Check out:

The Message
New Revised Standard Version
English Standard Version
Good News Bible
New International Version
New Living Bible
New Jerusalem Bible
(There are several other versions, and most are available in electronic format for tablets, Kindles etc.)

Read a few sample paragraphs, then decide which suits you. You may prefer to buy only a New Testament or even just one Gospel. Having chosen your Bible or New Testament, grab a quiet place; a good chair and a prayer that says:

'Jesus, this is your book. By your Spirit show me yourself. I am open to you.'

You're good to go.

So where do you start? Here's how I got started.

APPROACH IT WITH JESUS

Start with Jesus. Start with one Gospel.

Which one? Again, you look and choose.

Mark is the shortest and the fastest moving; thought to be dictated by Peter, this shows us Jesus the action-man Servant of God and people. Luke is the longest and the most flowing narrative; probably the best picture of Jesus the man. Matthew, slightly shorter than Luke, was written to show Jesus as the promised King of the Jews; with many links with the Old Testament. John, written some years after the others, paints a portrait of the man who was God, giving the inside track on him, his teaching, and training his disciples.

Whichever one you choose, read it as fast as you can – most of us can read a few chapters a day if we try. While you read, carry on praying 'Jesus make yourself real to me'. Read that Gospel three or four times, and where God speaks to you through it, mark the page with a highlighter or bookmark. When you hit problems, make notes so you can ask someone else about them, and carry on reading. Don't be afraid to make notes all over the pages if that helps. Just make it **your** Bible.

Then read all four – Matthew through to John three or four times. By now you will be really getting to know the God-man Jesus. So when you reach the end of John on the third or fourth occasion keep going straight on to the end of Revelation. Remember this book is a love letter from the Father-Maker to you. Through it he will speak to you as his son/daughter, as he never quite spoke to anyone before. This is your destiny – don't let go of it.

When you have read the New Testament three or four times you will be ready to tackle the Old Testament!

It's helpful to remember that roughly half of the Old Testament is taken up by the historical books: Genesis to Esther. The other half is made up by poetical books: Job to Song of Solomon and the prophets Isaiah to Malachi. You could start at Genesis and Job changing the mood day by day. Whatever you do, don't drop the reading of the New Testament. Carry on getting to know Jesus and he will keep on leading you. When you feel discouraged remember just three chapters a day will take you through the Bible in one year!

APPROACH IT IN FREEDOM

If that makes you feel worse then chill out, stop worrying and keep on reading at the rate that suits you. Whatever you do, keep on reading and receiving the Holy Spirit so he can take the scriptures and make Jesus real to you in a new and never-to-be-repeated way. Alternatively, try the various 'One Year Bibles'.

Once when some intellectuals asked him a foolish question Jesus replied,

> 'You're off base on two counts: you don't know your Bibles, and you don't know how God works.'[7]

Without knowing our Bibles, we all run the risk of being as stupid as they were.

Even worse, without knowing the Bible you will find it almost impossible to keep your feet on the path of your destiny, the reason for your living, the fulfilment of all you are.

So what are you waiting for? Boldly go…!

> 'Jesus,
> you are the Word of God.
> Open my eyes to see you in the Bible.
> By your Spirit be real to me.
> Never let me be ignorant of the scriptures
> or of God's power.
> Thank you for helping me.
> Amen.'

The Word of God has another title: the sword of the Spirit. We need such a weapon because of the real battle in which we are involved. Locked in combat in a heavenly war we must learn to use heavenly weapons. Let's turn to the subject of prayer, the Christian's information superhighway.

CHAPTER 9
TOUCHING HEAVEN
– CHANGING EARTH

'And war broke out in heaven... and the great dragon was thrown down, that ancient serpent, who is called the Devil and Satan, the deceiver of the whole world – he was thrown down...'[1]

PRAYER IS VITAL

When we looked at the Adam and Eve story, we saw how their surrender to Satan brought them under his control. Not only that, the earth that was placed under their authority by the Creator, was immediately yielded to Satan's power. So God's world has been stolen by the enemy. Father God wants his ball back! The moment we joined with Jesus, we also signed up to his Army of Liberation. We are at war!

It's a titanic struggle between the God of heaven and the Prince of darkness. Right now it's raging across the face of the globe, unseen because it is a spiritual war taking place in the heavenly realms. That makes it even more real than physical warfare. In it our prayers are decisive. For many people, the two words 'prayer meeting' possibly constitute the most boring phrase ever invented. Yet **real** prayer is the most exciting activity the world has ever known. Prayer is the way we enter the invisible realities of that heavenly realm Our contribution is vital.

The victory of Golgotha, when Jesus representing us confronted the full power of Satan and defeated it, was the climax, not the end. To his Bride, the Church, he has given the privilege of completing the final downfall of Satan. God has given her his authority. Even before the coming of Christ men knew what it was to see miracles by prayer...

1. PRAYER IS WARFARE

Some malicious will was at work within Israel.[2] There was continual grumbling, and quarrels seemed to break out with little reason. Few understood why they must journey through the starkness of the wilderness to the holy mountain: Horeb – Mount Sinai, standing in an area of jumbled rocky peaks in the wilderness of Paran. Moses knew 'someone' was opposing the people of Yahweh, in their march southwards to meet their God at Sinai. Confirmation was there in the solid shape of the Amalekite army.

They'd heard of Israel's escape from Egypt and their God's call to return to the land he'd promised them. They feared Israel would attack them on the way to Canaan. So they mobilised their army to meet and defeat them far south and west of their own borders. Today would be the decisive battle. Just before dawn, Moses and some attendants climbed the highest hill in the area. The whole valley lay before them. As the sun tipped over the horizon its first rays touched the summit of Sinai far to the south. Moses' pulse quickened. Win this battle and the way would be open. There the holy presence waited. He turned back to the valley below, still in darkness.

Joshua had roused the men early, and was even now deploying his forces for assault on the Amalekite positions. The sun rose swiftly, spilling light into the valley. Standing on the edge of the hill, Moses silhouette could clearly be seen. He raised his hands – in them the rod of God: symbol of holy power. Suddenly the blare of trumpets. Attack!

The Israeli signal was answered by Amalekite buglers: 'To arms!' The inexperienced soldiers of Israel now faced the accomplished Amalekite army. This would be a make or break day. If they were defeated here in their first battle, they might never survive as a nation.

And Moses knew it.

2. PRAYER IS HARD WORK

He knew their real hope was not in the new young recruits, advancing over ground slippery with blood, hideous with severed limbs and spattered brains. Their hope was in God's authority. Sweat streamed down his aching arms as he held up the rod. Whenever he dropped his arms, the battle started to go against Israel. He knew he must stand with hands raised in triumph over the battle until it was won. Now his arms were trembling with exhaustion. Still the battle raged on.

Aaron and Hur realised they must do something to help Moses go on proclaiming God's power. They moved a huge stone into position so that Moses could sit. Then they each took one arm and held his hands up in the position of authority and victory. The Amalekites were mown down, their remnants broke and fled, the way was open.

Before they left, Moses erected an altar and called it 'The Banner of the Lord'. He said he had put 'a hand on the banner of the Lord'. What a great description of prayer. A banner is the sign of the King's presence and authority. But remember, this kind of prayer had its roots in Moses' relationship with God. At the burning bush they'd met – and their conversation continued until the day Moses died. He knew God as no man ever did.

3. PRAYER IS INTIMACY WITH GOD

But then, that's our calling. Ever since the coming of the Holy Spirit, all who trust in Christ can know the Father with the same intimacy as Moses: know him as no one else ever did. We discover our identity in relationship with others, fixing the shape and borders of our own personality. This is truest of all in our relationship with God. We bring our own special individual nature to him and find its meaning in knowing him. So the first function of prayer is to enter relationship with the Father. The Lord's Prayer begins with relationship: 'Our Father in heaven'. Your first aim must be to know him – and let him know you.

Yet prayer often becomes a barrier. Some people feel they should only pray in a certain position or place, or at a certain special time. Others use special words, even a special tone of voice. Such things are barriers to real relationship. God has called you to know him, to find something in him that no one ever knew before. He is Father and understands you better than anyone.

So relax. If you find it hard to pray sitting or kneeling, walk around the room – the park, or the hills. Tell him the truth, the utter truth about yourself. Use normal language and bring him your feelings: joy, thankfulness, grief, frustration, boredom. Even rage at him, he is a very big Daddy – he can take it!

Opening up to him you will find him beginning to fill up empty places, to heal ancient wounds and release entrenched pain. 'God' and 'Father' will cease to be empty words; they'll become a person known and beloved. His constant love will increasingly set you free to be who you are. You'll come to know your real value.

From the moment he met God at the burning bush, Moses was a man being changed. It started when God said,

> *'Take off your sandals, for you are standing on holy ground.'*[3]

Not that Moses' shoes were defiling holy ground. God was saying, 'no barriers between us'. In real prayer, we walk with no shoes, on God's road – sometimes a road strewn with thorns.

4. PRAYER IS TRANSFORMING

Intimacy in prayer transforms us. Getting to know the God of heaven we are tinged by his radiance. The child begins to look like the Father. So give him a chance. Spend time in his presence. In our tense frantic world it takes time and practise to relax. But it's worth investing in knowing God. Learn just to be in his presence and to know his majesty as God, all around you, the great stillness of his peace – peace beyond all our understanding. Someone who has received the Father's peace is rare, beautiful and refreshing.

This kind of transformation is your God-given right. You can be what you are meant to be – not only because of Jesus' sacrifice in history, but because he now stands before the throne of God, hearing and knocking back every accusation Satan brings against you. He's your defence lawyer. Every time Satan accuses you of sin, Jesus reminds our holy God that his death covered your sin; like a rich friend covering the debts of a bankrupt. In addition he comes to remind you that his Father is your Father.

5. PRAYER IS FOR ALL

Before Jesus came, men of a certain family were appointed as priests – middle men between God and the people. They carried that privilege as long as they lived. Jesus' death and ascension changed all that. The rebellion and fall lost its power. People could once more walk with God. The Bible declares all Christians are priests – there's no longer a special class. Some churches may ask ministers to carry that title. It's a reminder of the function of all Christians. But Jesus the man is the only intermediary now needed. That's why you can truly know God the Father. His son stands between you linking you to each other.

Once you have received the life of the Son of God, you've become a child of God, and an heir of God's kingdom. You're a partner in the family business. As great High Priest Jesus appoints you to join him in his priesthood; standing before the throne of God, bearing the needs and torment of a world in chains.

This is a massive function of prayer. It is no good saying this is only for special people – he'll simply reply that you are special. This high calling is your destiny.

6. PRAYER TOUCHES OTHERS

Certain people are closer to you than any other Christian; your wife, husband, children, parents, relatives, siblings, girlfriend, boyfriend, fiancée, neighbours and workmates. The thrilling opportunity of priesthood is yours. Job had seven sons and three daughters. He was rich. They enjoyed a full life, including many parties which could last for days. Job used to get up early, the morning after each party, to pray God would forgive each child for any foolish or careless sin. He knew that it was a Father's job to act as a priest to each family member. You have the right to pray for others that God's will shall be done in their lives. It's part of the reason why God made you. He knew that through your prayers, he could touch certain people he could reach no other way. How amazing to be part of unfolding God's will in someone else's life. All Christians have this power. As redeemed heirs of Adam, we have authority in heaven.

In praying, we draw the power of **heaven** into earth. This is our mission – linking a loving almighty God to the oppressed of the world. We stand for them before him. God sees us, empowers our prayers with his Spirit and loves to answer.

7. PRAYER OPENS THE DOOR TO HEALING

The heat in the little house near the sea was almost unbearable. People from every village of Galilee were crowded in to listen to the teacher. The best seats were taken by rows of local ministers and Bible students who sat listening hour after hour; occasionally smiling, sometimes muttering to each other, their brows knit in disapproval.

A steady stream of sick and injured people were brought for healing. There had been many miracles. But now the crush made it impossible to get through. The crowd filled the grounds of the house and the street outside.

A paralysed man lay on his stretcher listening to the arguments, as his friends tried to force a way through the solid mass. It was no good. He felt sure this was part of his punishment. He had sinned, God knew. He didn't deserve to be healed. His friends gave up trying to get in and started back down the street. The stretcher rocked uneasily as they pushed against the flow of the crowd.

It went quiet. Raising his head he could see they were moving down a narrow side street. Then he understood. They planned to approach the house from a different direction. Finally close to the house, the stretcher was lowered to the ground. When they explained the plan he was certain they were crazy! Surely the teacher wouldn't thank them for dropping in like this! They were great guys.

Riding their shoulders up the steps at the side of the house was worrying. Worse was listening to them breaking up the tiles and the roof. But he'd never forget swaying uneasily over the heads of the crowd as they lowered the stretcher into the room. Then the teacher was looking at him. He felt his sins showed as if they were scrawled in scarlet letters on his face. Utter hopelessness gripped him. When he raised his eyes again, the teacher wasn't looking at him but at the grinning faces peering through the hole in the roof. 'You can do it, Master', one said. 'Nobody knows what's wrong with him – but you can heal him', said another.

Again the teacher looked down. His eyes were piercing… pain-filled.

'Your sins are forgiven.'

A moment of silence, then the babble of argument and protest broke out. No matter. He knew. Somehow in those seconds the teacher had taken the guilt from him. It had cost him too, he could see that. The argument continued. The teacher looked at him again.

'Listen to me, get up. Pick up your stretcher and go home.'

He did it – simple as that! Did it. Went home singing.

Jesus could do that because he saw 'their' faith. The man's friends didn't know it, but their action was priestly – costly in time and effort, demonstrating faith. They had brought a weak, guilty, paralysed man into the transforming presence of Christ. We're called to do the same.

8. PRAYER TOUCHES THE INVISIBLE

Another privilege. In prayer we touch hidden realities, dealing in issues more real than even physical pains. We touch eternal immensities. If only we would grasp the enormous possibilities. Imagine 'ordinary' Christians daring to receive from God, blessings on behalf of others – and passing them on by faith. We can do it in the absence of the person in need, and without their knowing. Why not dare to do it? Stand before God, hold out your hands, cupped to receive blessing on behalf of anyone on your heart – then pass it on by faith. Do it consistently, believing in his power, and **watch them** being transformed. It's exciting – to see God's power working here on planet Earth, as you claim God's blessing on your area of authority, by faith. This is real. It is dealing with the God of heaven on the basis of his promises. It works. Faith in action.

9. PRAYER TOUCHES THE WORLD OF SUFFERING AND PAIN

Just look around the world for a few moments. Consider what sin has done. That awful moment in Eden when Eve was promised insight, knowledge and freedom has resulted in blindness, ignorance and bondage for the whole human race. Tonight, two-thirds of the world will go to bed hungry. Probably twenty thousand will die of starvation. Others will endure another night of misery and pain as multiple sclerosis, muscular dystrophy, leukaemia, cancers, Aids, malaria, leprosy and countless other diseases and infections continue their relentless cull of humanity.

There are casualties of war: victims of historical conflicts, World Wars I and II, Hiroshima and scarred children of napalm attacks in Vietnam; conflict in Afghanistan, Syria, Israel and Palestine; and always refugees in their millions. Nuclear accidents, earthquakes, tsunamis, forest fires, floods and tornadoes. Think of the terrible private suffering of the mentally ill, or those addicted to drugs, alcohol, gambling and pornography. It's a world of torment and pain. Then there are those brought under direct satanic tyranny – by involvement in Ouija boards, spiritualism, tarot, black/white magic, as well as deliberate acts of rebellion against God. As Gandalf said in *Lord of the Rings*, 'I pity even his slaves'.

Ponder this empire of misery. Surely our hearts and minds revolt against its hellish author, and long to restore the rightful King. No wonder David said, *'I hate God's enemies with a perfect hatred'*. That's the right direction for all our anger at suffering – against Satan and his demonic hordes of deceiving spirits.

> *'For our fight is not against any physical enemy: it is against organisations and powers that are spiritual. We are up against the unseen power that controls this dark world, and spiritual agents from the very headquarters of evil.'*[4]

So this is prayer – how can we think it's boring? In particular this is the purpose of praying together: to stand against all the power of hell and win.

10. PRAYER IS MILITANT ACTION

Another area where we are called to exercise priesthood is praying for our nation. We begin by bringing before God areas of national guilt; accepting them as ours, and pleading for forgiveness through the blood of Christ. Our exploitation of third and fourth world countries; refusal to defend the weak and persecuted; the toll of innocent lives under our abortion laws; the pollution of our environment with all the rubbish of a selfish materialistic society; the spiritual and moral pollution of pornography – devaluing women and degrading men. If we are not to sink beneath the weight of our own guilt, we must carry our nation's guilt to the cross of Christ. That is our task.

Then by faith we need to spend even more time releasing God's blessing upon our government (whatever we think of them!) The Law, Police, commercial and industrial sector, entertainment industry, sports and voluntary sector. Satan loves to **condemn**. Let's rejoice to **bless**.

We are also called to be an army of **priests**, touching heaven with prayer so the whole body of Christ is touched and constantly renewed by heavenly power. Of course, there's a problem. Satan won't let this happen if he can possibly prevent it. He is mortally afraid of the Church, continually gnawed by fear. He knows far better than we do the enormous authority vested in her by her Lord.

Revelation calls us priests **and** kings. In Old Testament thought, kings were warriors called to do battle with any encroaching enemy, turn him back and expand the territory of God's people. We are called to be **warrior kings**. In New Testament times, kings were expected to reign – that is, exhibit regal authority, controlling their kingdom by strength of character.

Enemy strongholds in our country and across the world will never be destroyed – except by prayer filled with the power of the 'Lord of Hosts', the God of battles. Intentionally do that, and at last we'll be acting as kings and priests. The nation will begin to feel the impact of our prayers. Think about the entrenched powers of private and institutional greed:

- Vicious and ruthless exploiters of the vulnerable
- Groomers, abusers, and traffickers of the young
- Anti-human purveyors of sexual perversion and indulgence
- Merchants of pornography
- Drug dealers
- Those serving money and power who subject others to tyranny
- All who offer liberty and only deliver greater bondage

Their roots and hidden power are under the spiritual domination of Satan.

To attack such powers locally and nationally, we must learn to act together as warrior priests. We must hit the enemy where it hurts – in his power base. Fear. That's what gives him power. We have something that drives out fear – love that's mature. Add to that the joy of praising God, thanksgiving and laughter. That kind of prayer is not limited to any local area: not even to this world, galaxy or universe. Real prayer, specifically directed to exalt our supremely happy, holy Trinity, drives Satan crazy. When we magnify the Loving Father, the victorious Son and the dancing Holy Spirit, our exaltation of our God will seek him, find him and hit him wherever in creation he tries to hide. When we pour all our fascination and adoration on our God, we starve our enemy of what he craves – our attention.

11. PRAYER USES GOD'S EQUIPMENT

> 'Therefore you must wear the whole armour of God that you may be able to resist evil in its day of power, and that even when you have fought to a standstill you may still stand your ground.'[5]

We live in a world claimed and often controlled by the enemy. We must use the right equipment to be able to resist his assaults. He will attack us. He knows he must beat us or lose everything. He'll attack our honesty, morals, stability and our peace of mind. He will constantly try to bring us to despair.

> *'Take your stand then with truth as your belt, righteousness your breastplate, the gospel of peace firmly on your feet, salvation as your helmet, and in your hand the sword of the Spirit, the Word of God. Above all, be sure you take faith as your shield, for it can quench every burning missile the enemy hurls at you.'*[6]

As well as the sword of the Spirit, Paul also commands the Ephesians to go on the offensive against the enemy with *'all prayer'* *'with thanksgiving'*.[7] God has given the world and its dominion into the hands of its people. He needs people to voluntarily yield it back to him. That is the purpose of the prayer, *'Let your kingdom come'*. It's a strange prayer because in it we get to command God to release his Kingdom into our earth. Of course, its power depends on our faith and persistence, and our agreement in prayer with the body of Christ.

12. PRAYER GRASPS GOD'S WEAPONS

We have been given certain very simple but effective weapons. These weapons are effective against all the power of the enemy as they are used under the instructions of the Holy Spirit. When praying against evil powers, we must commit ourselves to the control of the Spirit of Christ. The Holy Spirit will first lead us to magnify and praise God. Only then will we see enemy strongholds destroyed. For as Paul wrote, the weapons of our warfare are mighty to destroy strongholds.

First among them is **the Bible itself**. As we quote this we know at the very least it is utterly true and inspired. Mind you, Satan is not above misusing it himself to confuse us. He did it to Jesus in the wilderness.[8] And Jesus used it right back, exalting the Father's authority. The Bible is a sword – so use it. Take its words. Thrust them at the powers of darkness. They will feel them and shrink back.

Another weapon is **the blood of Christ** – the sign of his victorious death and our forgiveness; having great power to lift oppression from us, and to release people from satanic bondage. Before any group sets out to pray against some stronghold of the enemy, it is vital that they consciously claim the cleansing of the death of Jesus.

Then there is **the cross of Christ**. Reminding the Devil of it has two values: there in Christ, I was crucified and died, thus passing out of Satan's control; and it's the place of Satan's own total defeat. **The name of Jesus** is also a mighty weapon. We use that name conscious of its great authority. Paul declares that every knee will bow at the name of Jesus, because God gave his own name, 'Lord', '*the name above every name*', to Jesus Christ.

We must never forget to receive the anointing of **the Holy Spirit** so the enemy always sees us covered with him, like the wrestlers of ancient Greece who covered themselves in oil. It made them hard to get hold of, and almost impossible to pin down. The Holy Spirit gives Satan the same problem.

TOUCHING HEAVEN, CHANGING EARTH

This is a vast and much-neglected subject. All I can do is to skim the surface. So I'm finishing this vital topic with a brief review. Jesus taught us to pray, *'Let your kingdom come, let your will be done on earth as it is in heaven.'* We are to speak out certain prayers like a monarch giving an order. To God! We are Children of the King, training to reign with him.

God gave this world to humans. Adam and Eve rebelled. Satan became their Master and ruled their world. Only other humans can reverse the decision they made. Then this planet will be restored to its rightful owner – God. The prayer Jesus gives us expects us to act like people of royal power. We are to take authority and tell our Creator to *'let'* his Kingdom come. We're saying, 'Release your kingdom – let it go that it may eagerly fill the earth. Release your will so that our earth will be remade in beauty, creation restored and we humans be filled at last with glory.'

All the power of God gets in behind such prayers. When enough of the human race prays like this, I believe Jesus will return. Our voice may be weak – but holy reality pours through such declarations to fill them with power, and clothe them with authority. Our proclamation builds a pathway for Jesus. One day the King will come. Prayer really matters. Surely our prayers should be fresh-filled by a spirit of aggression and confidence against the enemy.

Before we attempt to do anything in this fallen world – whether feeding the hungry, lifting the oppressed, or preaching the good news – we should first saturate the scene in authoritative prayer, in the power of the Holy Spirit, magnifying and praising Jesus over it all, rejoicing in his victory. Prayer like this is the most practical thing we can do.

Reminder: we're talking about heavenly warfare. There is an enemy, and he will do his best to fight back. Such prayer may be costly. This kind of spiritual offensive usually needs two or three people. Work with others. By such prayer, situations are changed, mountains moved, people blessed – and God is glorified. Our destiny is to *reign in life through the one man Jesus Christ*. We are meant to live, not as hopeless failures, but as warrior kings – encouraging our brothers and sisters, glorifying God and terrifying Satan.

This is **your** destiny: to exercise God's authority as his representative in the enemy-held territory of this world. For this the Creator himself fathered you, loved and chose you before the world was made, or the stars were formed.

There is an area of life which is uniquely yours. You are primarily responsible for it. Don't dare think God would not entrust something to you. Every human being has spiritual responsibility for something. In the parable of the talents, the master gave every servant a talent for which they were then responsible to him.[9] Only *you* can pray the authority of God down into your corner of the world. No one else can. All heaven is trembling at the rim of the world, watching. The saints of the past are cheering you on. So 'boldly go' to extend God's authority 'where no one has gone before'.

Jesus has promised to walk with you. He will.

'Lord,
teach me to pray.
In my best moments
I long to spend hours with you.
Then I find something else to do.
Forgive me.
Help me discover what real prayer is.
Train me in intimacy.
Let me enter your heart.
Lead me into adoration.
Teach me to pray.
Amen.'

God's purpose for you and me goes far beyond the frontiers of space and time, into eternity. In the next chapter we try to glimpse where that may take us.

CHAPTER 10
THE
LAST
BATTLE

'The whole fury and might of the enemy must very soon be turned on us. Hitler knows that he must break us in this island or lose the war. Let us therefore brace ourselves to our duties, and so bear ourselves that if the British Empire and its Commonwealth last for a thousand years, men will still say, *"This was their finest hour"*.'[1]

HISTORY POINTS FORWARD

It's a long time ago now – June 1940, when Winston Churchill spoke these words. The armies of Adolf Hitler seemed invincible. Few people expected Britain to be able to resist them. Even less outside of Britain would have given 'the British Empire and its Commonwealth' more than another year of life. Yet filled with faith in 'Providence', and inspired by the trust of King George VI, Churchill could look at the possibility that it would last for a thousand years.

Now, that Empire – like all proud empires – has faded away. Adolf Hitler, George VI and Winston Churchill are all dead and have receded into history books. 'That's the way it is.' All human structures – political or physical, all leaders – good or evil, finally fade away and die. Yet they are not meaningless. They point to an eternal reality. All who are in Christ are already part of that reality.

THE KINGDOM OF GOD IS FOREVER...

We herald another King – Jesus. We serve a nobler empire, and inhabit a commonwealth richer than any earthly empire could ever be. It cannot be measured in billions of years. It is eternal – the kingdom of heaven. And we are citizens, members of its imperial family. Our kingdom of love is not built like this world's empires, on the backs of helpless slaves. Instead, it's made of one great family born into Christ, becoming like him.

...THE KINGDOM OF DARKNESS OPPOSES

But as we've seen, this world lies in the hands of another ruler – the Prince of Darkness. Because of Christ's victory at Calvary he knows he is defeated. He cannot win. Desperately, he clings to a last vain hope. The final blow will be struck against him from this earth. So if he can prevent the Church from mounting that assault... All his energies therefore are directed against her. In his crafty scheming and deception there is one overriding strategy: defeat the Church – divide it, defile it, destroy it. The worldwide body of Christ is the island of God's kingdom on earth in an ocean of human societies dominated by materialism, greed, ethnic rivalries, demonic hatreds and religious pride. He knows he must break us in this island or irrevocably lose the war.

How long before he pours out his last reserves in a final assault? At the Mount of Olives the disciples asked Jesus about the end of the world. He told them that in the closing period of history, before his return as Lord, there would be a final world-wide and most terrible attack on the Church. A coordinated wave of persecution preceded by increasing unrest: ethnic wars, conflict between nations, and natural disasters, culminating in international alliances united in hatred of the Church and of Israel.

Such periods have occurred before. In history, people have identified Caesar, Napoleon, Mussolini and Hitler amongst others, as Satan's representative the Antichrist. But we should look carefully at our own era. After all, for one generation the return of Jesus Christ will cease to be in the future, and become instantly present reality. Maybe our generation will be the one!

OUR CULTURE IS COLLAPSING

If we look at the evidence in western society as a whole, we can see certain tendencies which, if they continue, will bring about the collapse of the liberal democracies.

No society can survive if all its pillars – religion, the family, law, government and work – are destroyed at the same time. In many countries, this process is now well advanced. History suggests if this goes on, collapse into chaos or violent and bloody revolution is hugely likely. The eventual outcome of such a collapse would be government by force. A totalitarian state – of any kind – would certainly put the church under dreadful pressure.

It's not the worst thing that could happen. Down the centuries, vast numbers of Christians have lived, as the greater part of the body of Christ lives today, under pressure or direct persecution. Because churches in that situation quickly learn what's really important, they are often healthier than the churches of the 'free' world.

Even so we are called to pray that the Lord will act in power in our nations, and in western society, to save us from destruction. Because although persecution produces a healthy Church, it hurts the weak, the young, the very old, and the vulnerable. May our loving God have mercy on us and give the Church a new heart, so that through her, great rivers of his love and life may be poured into the community, and our whole society be changed. It can happen. Powerful prayer and inspired presentation of Jesus have changed the course of history before. They can again.

THE NATIONS ARE IN TURMOIL

The world is increasingly troubled. When the Berlin Wall was demolished in late 1989, it seemed to usher in a new age. Other nations of the Soviet Union ousted old-style communist governments. But the USSR still seemed inviolable. Within two years the unthinkable had happened: the Union of Soviet Socialist Republics had disintegrated. It was a moment of optimism. What one US President called 'the Evil Empire' had vanished.

As the 'Soviet bloc' went down to history, far older hatreds emerged. Tribal and ethnic rivalries plunged large sections of that empire into chaos, violence and war, as if a great gravestone had been smashed, releasing old demons from the tainted earth. The world became much more unstable and dangerous. After a time of increasing uncertainty and anxiety, things appeared to settle. The new Millennium began with guarded optimism, that we might be entering a period of world peace and prosperity.

This did not fit in with the plans of Al Qaeda, a fundamentalist Muslim group led by Osama Bin Laden. At his command at 6.00 am on 11 September 2001, four teams of radical fundamentalist Muslims set in motion a plan to hijack four passenger planes. Two planes were crashed into the Twin Towers of the World Trade Centre in Manhattan, New York. One plunged into the Pentagon, another plummeted into the ground as heroic passengers wrestled with the hijackers for control of the plane – apparently intended for the Capitol in Washington. 2,977 people perished immediately. America, her allies and many neutral nations were appalled. It's horrible – but this single day achieved what Bin Laden wanted. It created war between radical Islam and the non-Muslim world. Intervention in Afghanistan by leading Western nations was a direct result. And the subsequent war in Iraq was a further consequence.

THE POWDER KEG IGNITES

Such foreign policy actions had an unintended side-effect. News from these wars and their ongoing conflicts ignited many young Muslims worldwide. Radicalised, they became ready recruits for Al Qaeda and other terrorist organisations. All over the Muslim world, tensions between tribal groups and different age groups escalated. The so-called 'Arab Spring' swept across North Africa, creating a domino effect as regimes fell in quick succession.

But democracy depends upon consensus. In a volatile and fluid situation, that kind of agreement must be created. Groups seen as outsiders make convenient scapegoats. Too often recently, that dynamic has coalesced around hatred and persecution of the Church. In many Muslim lands, our brothers and sisters are in mortal peril.

Meanwhile in other parts of our world, violence between national and tribal groupings is increasing – in Europe, Asia, India and Africa. Racial tensions continue to threaten the US. Nazis are back on the streets of Europe. National Socialism, whatever its national identity, is powerfully attractive to powerless and frightened people. Seeking to combat all this, fundamentalist liberals are increasingly intolerant, seeking to impose 'political correctness' in every area of life. In their opposition to racism, they're often at least as violent as the fascists. You become what you hate. It is the curse of our fallenness. Trying to do our best we're often at our worst. It seems hopeless. How should we respond?

Jesus told us,

> *'On the earth nations will be in anguish and perplexity at the roaring and tossing of the sea. Men will faint from terror, apprehensive of what is coming on the world, for the heavenly bodies will be shaken... When these things begin to take place, **stand up and lift up your heads** because your redemption is drawing near.'*[2]

Reading a prophecy like this, we can easily forget it's not just poetic language, but about real events. The 26 December 2004 Indian Ocean tsunami was caused by an earthquake thought to have realised the energy of 23,000 Hiroshima-type atomic bombs. 300,000 people died – approximately. Tsunamis cause huge amounts of damage and generate the kind of anguish and perplexity Jesus describes. Fascinating, sobering – and pointing forward to the day of his return. We should always be aware our redemption is drawing near.

VIOLENCE FILLS THE EARTH

Worldwide, growing violence within nations reflects the lessening influence of the specifically Jewish/Christian idea that every individual is valuable. This process is particularly noticeable in post-Christian societies like Britain and the US. On 2 August 1993, 'Time' chronicled what it called 'the deadly love affair between America's youth and firearms'; citing 'the inexplicable despair that torments so many American teenagers... some days, guns are just a defence against boredom that comes from a lack of guidance and direction'.

Twenty years later after an horrific massacre of primary school children, the President tried to reintroduce some measure of gun control. He failed. America's national story is written in the blood of those who rebelled against oppression. Across the heartland of America, suspicion of the federal government – fear of what is seen as "big government" is just too strong.

In Europe the same boredom is all too evident, with the same resort to violence. In the second decade of the twenty first Century we have seen violent, even murderous riots on the streets of European cities. Here in England, drug barons battle for control: gun battles in the streets – once unthinkable – occur regularly in some inner-city areas. Some of these are the result of hit squads from Eastern European Mafia groups "levelling the score". Men of violence recognise no boundaries. We don't have the time to look at these situations in detail, or at the rest of the world.

PEOPLE ARE BEYOND RESTRAINT

The flower children of the sixties and seventies left a poisoned legacy. 'If it feels good, do it' meant people opened the door to the tyranny of their own desires. Sex as sport, the search for pleasure, the worship of physical sensation, devalued any ideas of deferred gratification, real relationship or emotional commitment.

The lessening of restraints in 'the new morality' led only to deeper enslavement by the old immorality. In their pain and guilt, people saw rules of moral conduct as instruments of oppression. Any suggestion of sexual self-control was greeted as 'unhealthy repression'. The increasing affluence of the Western World was built on economic oppression of the developing world. It can only make things worse. God blessed us so we can bless others. We're living in luxury not earned by the equivalent amount of hard work. Believing in God, we must believe in accountability. His judgement hangs over us like a sword, suspended by a thread of mercy.

We brought up this generation of young people to expect instant gratification. They've learned well. Often more emotionally attached to a tablet or smart phone than a parent, they have a constant need for sensation, for visual stimulation. Denied the opportunity for real struggle, and the satisfaction of achievement, too often untrained in constructive expression, they may release their energy in aggression and violence. Geared to interacting with screens, the most horrifying images dull their sensitivities to death and suffering.

Others see on their screens flawless images of attractiveness they can never quite attain. Everywhere they turn they see air-brushed perfection. The media are all around them. No escape. Eating disorders are inevitable as some seek to reach the elusive ideal image. Others sink into despair overeating morbidly – literally eating themselves to death. Demanding instant solutions to complex problems, most are the spoilt grandchildren of consumerism. Empty and frustrated, they are easy prey for drug pushers, and for cheap alcohol – some becoming problem drinkers before they are teenagers. We've given them everything –

except what they really need: inner meaning, a reason to live, a focus outside themselves, faith in the eternal God.

SEXUAL CORRUPTION SPREADS

Meanwhile, in our obedience to the 'anything goes' sexual ethic, we have opened the way for children to become victims of the most perverted fantasies. We have failed to acknowledge, one man's 'freedom of expression' may become another's exploitation. Some academics even try to provide an apologetic for paedophiles saying 'they really care' for their victims. I don't deny that even a child molester can have human feelings. But only a depraved human has any involvement with children five or six years old being sexually abused. Meanwhile, in the sex markets of Bangkok, tiny children are being abused dozens of times a day (mostly by European, American and Japanese men).

A vast pornographic industry provides a constant stream of perversion, stimulating these men, downloads that glorify bondage, sado-masochism and rape. It degrades children and exploits women, while building up hatred of the female in men who watch. It encourages rapists and sex murderers as it did Peter Sutcliffe, the 'Yorkshire Ripper'. Decades later, in early 2013 two dreadful UK cases of child rape and murder resulted in convictions. Both men were obsessed with images of children being raped. Neither of them had any previous convictions of sexual offences. Tia Sharpe and April Jones paid an horrendous price for the licence extended to pornographers. Yet the arts and media establishment is, by and large, more concerned with defending freedom of expression than condemning this muck. So sexual corruption increasingly defiles our society.

THE CHALLENGE OF THE FAITHS

Sikhs, Hindus, and especially Muslims regard the Western world as the Christian world. Some of the finest representatives of those faiths live among us. They often show a commitment to prayer, and stability of family life, that put us to shame. Hindu and Sikh communities practise hospitality, offering food I envy for the Church! Many Islamists claim to offer the best alternative to the moral corruption of the Western world. Yet Islam's attitude to women is often oppressive; and violence is endorsed by Mohammed as a method of advancing their faith.

Undeniably, Christendom's history is full of gratuitous violence, often justified by religious teaching – for example the Crusades. But such shameful violence is totally contrary to the teaching of Jesus. His aim was a worldwide community of grace and love, flavouring every society with God's forgiveness and compassion. There is no such thing as a 'Christian nation'.

The recent resurgence of Islam seems likely to continue, fuelled by the vast oil riches of some Arab states. But power is hard to control. Tribal rivalries and the ancient antagonisms of Sunni and Shiite and have re-emerged with greater bitterness than ever. All Islamic nations are theoretically part of one body, Dar al Islam 'the house of Islam'. However, only one issue truly unites them: hatred of the state of Israel. 'My enemy's enemy is my friend,' echoes powerfully in Islam.

There is broad agreement on another issue – opposition to the church of Jesus Christ. The way this works out varies greatly in different nations. But most Muslim clergy and teachers would agree it is impossible to be a proper Muslim unless the whole community is governed by Islamic principles taken from the Koran. Classical Islam is a power-system aimed at total control of society. There is no room for individual decisions on important issues like religion. Christian evangelism, therefore, is deeply offensive to them. But Jesus has commanded us to evangelise everyone. Everywhere!

ISRAEL AT THE CENTRE OF EVENTS

The Bible affirms Jesus as Alpha and Omega: the A and Z, the beginning and end. Through Him all things were made and will be brought to fulfilment. Creation, and consummation are in Him. It's always been part of our faith to affirm, 'Christ will come again'. Some people have so spiritualised this that it no longer means what it says. But the meaning Jesus himself gave it remains. He, the eternal Son of God made flesh, will return to this earth from his place of authority in the heavenlies. He will come with great supernatural power and glory – instantly recognisable to the church and the world. He will come to usher in the kingdom of God on earth in its hour of greatest torment.

There are many doctrinal interpretations of this event. I don't intend to pick my way through that minefield! However most systems agree on one thing: the return of Jesus Christ is somehow tied up with the rebirth of Israel. Jesus himself linked the two, saying Jerusalem would be 'trodden down' by non-Jewish peoples, until the times of 'the Gentiles' **'comes to an end'**.[3] Israel's founding in 1948 is therefore crucial – but even more significant is 1967, the year of the Six-Day War. Then Israel took back Jerusalem, in the words of Israeli leaders, 'for ever'. Obviously the day the Israelis took Jerusalem, something shifted in the heavenlies.

Israel's position in our world seems likely to become increasingly isolated. The Western nations have modified their support for her, because of the oil weapon held by Islamic countries in Arabia and the Middle East. Israel appears to be the eye of a huge storm system. Sometimes the storm rages, sometimes it calms. One day it may engulf the whole world.

THE CHURCH UNDER THREAT

Clearly the 'coming of the Lord' is tied up with a pattern of events. It's not difficult to see the possibility of that pattern emerging as we look at the world scene. Maybe at last the travail of the earth is about to bring to birth the Lord's return. In any birth, there are false alarms and 'false labours'. These can produce a feeling, 'the baby will never come' – but it does. There have been other moments in history when people felt the Return was imminent and were disappointed. This doesn't mean that he's not on the way.

We need to think soberly and with open minds, avoiding both hysteria and cynicism.

It may be our generation will see the veil hiding heaven from earth torn apart to allow the Prince on his white horse to ride through, defeat the forces of the enemy, and take the Church – his bride – to be with Him. On the brink of this longed-for event, the Church will almost certainly enter the hour of its deepest trial, its most terrible suffering: the time of universal persecution. It could be us. It seems improbable that such persecution could arise in an easy-going society in which 'tolerance' is the greatest virtue. Yet right there is the issue that may trigger our trial. Christians are bound to honour all people, respecting their right to believe as they choose, and acknowledging whatever truth may be in other faiths. But we are committed to Jesus Christ as **the Truth**. Where other religions differ from Jesus, we have to say – lovingly, respectfully but firmly, those faiths are mistaken. Jesus Christ is the Way, the Truth and the Life.

Like Abraham, people may come to know the living God outside of Christian revelation; or like Naaman, worship outside it. They can only know God as Father through Jesus. This forces people to decide for him – or against him. It makes them uncomfortable. The truth remains. He's not just Lord for his followers. He is Lord of **all**. Such an affirmation – no matter how courteous its expression, will offend those whose only absolute truth is that there is no absolute truth. Persecution would come to us.

What are we to do then?

GOD IS STILL IN CONTROL

First, recognise that God makes no mistakes. When such a time of pressure comes and you are to live through it, it's because he has chosen you to stand for him in the now. It's a privilege. Remember this last short time of pain for the Church will be its 'finest hour'. One of the great honours of eternity will be to have stood for Jesus Christ in this moment. The Bible proclaims such people carry special glory. If it comes in our time, let's rejoice!

Jesus said:

> *'Happy are those who are persecuted because they do what God requires; the kingdom of heaven belongs to them! Happy are you when people insult you and persecute you and tell all kinds of evil lies against you because you are my followers. Be happy and glad, for a great reward is kept for you in heaven.'*[4]

In such a situation understand God has chosen you – His special unique child – to represent Him. In the middle of cruelty and pain, the world will know there is a loving Father-Creator, and Jesus Christ is the one sent by him. This is your privilege and destiny, always. So be glad!

Be glad anyway! Even if the Lord's return is delayed for a thousand years, you have the unrepeatable privilege of being you. Gladly live that out, every day. Be an original – not a boring stereotype, copying other 'standard' Christians. We are not modules, but children. Father God rejoices in our individuality. It delights him. That's why he made us. Jesus was the most original person the world has ever known. And you are called to be like him, to live under the loving guidance of the Father, becoming truly yourself. So take up his banner, his commands and promises. Make them your own. Then go out into the world to live as nobody ever lived before.

'O Lord,
No way do I want to be persecuted,
or live in great tribulation
But when hard times come,
I will trust you.
You will carry me through.
You will bring me through darkness,
pain and suffering,
Into the joy of your kingdom.
I will come into your glorious Light
and live with you for ever.
Therefore, give me grace to obey you always.
Through Jesus who suffered,
and entered magnificent glory,
May I do the same.
Amen.'

CHAPTER 11
WHERE NO ONE HAS GONE BEFORE

'What is heaven to me, Lord? Surely it is nothing other than Jesus my God. For if heaven is that which is above all things, Then Lord God, you alone are heaven to my soul.'

Walter Hilton, Ladder of Perfection 1

HEAVEN WAITS FOR US

We are on the greatest journey possible – a voyage far beyond the bounds of our wildest imagining. We are on our way into the heart of God. He has declared his intention to unveil to us the endless mysteries – not only of creation, but of heaven; the realm of his reality, the unending vistas of his glory. Beyond the dark doorway of death, eternity stretches like a vast unexplored continent full of adventures waiting to be lived.

One further word about death. We may naturally dread the process of dying: the sudden shock of accident, the descent into cancer's pain, the long decline of degenerative disease. Though I believe we should pray for a 'good death'. Hebrews says, *'In that death, by God's grace, he (Jesus) fully experienced death in every person's place.'*[2] Whatever death awaits us, in the mysterious agony of the cross Jesus has tasted it for us already. He waits in the doorway to be our companion through it, and to bring us into the entrance to the heavenly city.

We seem to have suffered a loss of nerve about heaven. We don't speak of it with the glad conviction that Jesus offers. Are we too focused on the unfolding discoveries of the amazing creation around us? Heaven is greater and more magnificent than anything ever discovered – or yet to be discovered – in the material universe. That is certain. We need that certainty, to be free to live in this world as we should.

WE ARE CHILDREN OF THE ETERNAL FAMILY

The Holy Spirit, like a great-winged mother bird, broods over our planet. This world is yet to be won over by the love of Christ. The Father-Maker yearns for the estranged peoples of the earth. He longs to wrap the wounded billions in his care. Thus, our first calling is to be his child. God didn't create human doings – but human beings. The most important thing about you is not your function in the world or the church, but **who you are** in God. As you grow in that identity, you will increasingly be able to relate to others in Christ. Joined to each other, we discover the power of the body of Christ. Together we can accomplish what we could never do alone. United, we find more power for service, inspiration in worship and mutual protection in the heavenly war. Then in the security of family relationship with him and each other, we are able to go into all the world with the love and good news of Jesus.

Look at these marvellous words from Revelation:

> 'They defeated him through the blood of the Lamb, and the bold word of their witness. They weren't in love with themselves; they were willing to die for Christ'[3]

That is the purpose of your testimony – to conquer the enemy – but not alone! In this verse the word 'they' is used three times. Satan's defeat is something that is only accomplished corporately. We need each other; but the actions mentioned must be done individually. So the defeat of Satan can only come when Christians band together to stand individually against him. Your private victory will benefit your brother. My lonely defeat will weaken my sister. We stand as individuals joined in united action – a single body with many members: the body of Christ.

WE ARE MEMBERS TOGETHER OF ONE CHURCH

Just as we need each other as individuals, we need each other in our denominations and streams. No denomination in the church has a complete understanding or a perfect expression of God's revelation. Each denomination fills a gap in the understanding of others. The Anglicans need the House Churches, the Brethren need the Pentecostals, the Catholics need the Baptists, who need the Methodists...

Even within denominations there are differing views. Looking at the Gospels we can construct an Evangelical Jesus, a Liberal Christ, a Catholic Son of Man, or a Charismatic Son of God. Those portraits are all valid. Most of us can cope with one, two or even three of them. Four stretches us too far. The problem is – Jesus. He's always greater than our conceptions. He's impossible to contain. He is the living Lord. Only together as the whole Body of Christ, will we ever be able to show his full personality – together in time **and** eternity.

WE ARE SOLDIERS CALLED TO VICTORY

In the meantime, as the Revelation passage shows, we each have a part to play.

(i) Your destiny as an individual is to conquer the enemy: by on-going **willingness to repent**, receiving God's cleansing through the death of Christ. As God's sacrificial lamb he took all the blame for us, and carried our guilt. His blood – the sign of that death – is our defence whenever we are attacked by guilt or fear. I am forgiven. You are forgiven. The blood is the sign and guarantee of that forgiveness.

(ii) Your destiny is to conquer by your **witness to Jesus Christ**. No one else can know him as you do. So no one else can talk about him as you can. This is your own testimony: what Jesus Christ has done for you, and what he has become to you. Satan fears that kind of story because the revelation of your life in the kingdom of Jesus Christ proclaims to him his inevitable doom.

(iii) These weapons gain power to overcome Satan by the **commitment of your own life**. It's not just about words. We are talking about a new life lived under the authority and command of the living Lord Jesus. *'They loved not their lives even unto death'*, indicates the total commitment necessary to defeat Satan. Their lives – although important to them – were committed totally to Christ. They were prepared to die for the sake of Jesus. He mattered more.

When King Jesus reigns, there's no room for any other monarch – not even you! We can sing, 'He is Lord, He is Lord', but not realise how dangerous it is. When we sing it without meaning it, we invite that Lord to come and assess just how great His Lordship is in our lives. *'It's judgement time for Christians. We're first in line.'* [4] God is determined to get his family right, holy and happy before him. So discipline yourself. Be obedient to whatever Father God may ask. Live courageously as if your life doesn't matter compared to God's kingdom.

Whatever happens – boldly go!

Jesus has promised,

> *'Happy are those whose greatest desire is to do what God requires; God will satisfy them fully.'* [5]

WE WORSHIP A GREAT GOD... IN TIME...

This is a good point at which to stop and consider the ultimate aim of all that we have looked at. *'God will satisfy them fully'* because he is the great God. The Message reads, *'He (God) is food and drink in the best meal you'll ever eat.'* God's greatness seems to be missing from our consciousness. We know it in theory, but haven't been gripped by its reality.

Two words serve as a starting point for considering His greatness. They are missing from most modern Christianity, and their loss is responsible for much of our spiritual poverty. Majesty and Mystery. Majesty: God is the great King.

Maker and Ruler of all universes in all dimensions.

What we know of this universe beggars description. There is no way we can begin to encompass it in our minds. Our Earth is one of nine planets circling the Sun, which is one of over a hundred billion stars in the Milky Way, our home galaxy. The Milky Way is a fairly standard galaxy; some are much larger – others much smaller. Travelling at the speed of light (300,000 kilometres per second) it would take 100,000 years to cross it. To get to the furthest edge of the universe would take 200,000 times that – an unimaginable 20,000,000,000 years at the speed of light. Almost all the stars we can see in the sky are in our home galaxy, the Milky Way. Some 'stars' are actually distant galaxies. In this universe there are hundreds of billions of galaxies, each one an enormous star system in its own right.

He reigns over them all – the Lord in majesty. This aspect of his character is like an immeasurably, wide, deep river flowing full flood, irresistible in its course. To be aware of it is to be bathed in a great calm; the stillness of eternity. You are in the presence of immense and unimaginable strength. He is God of all gods, King of all kings, Maker of all things. The Bible calls him the everlasting Father. Vaster than we ever imagined, his greatness is not based on the physical splendour of his creation. He birthed that in a momentary explosion of energy and glory, which we still call 'the Big Bang'. His majesty and glory are derived entirely from who He is.

... AND IN ETERNITY

The Psalms declare, *'From everlasting to everlasting, you are God.'*[6] That's eternity: everlasting going forwards **and** backwards. God has always been; in relationship as Everlasting Father to his glorious Son, and with the eternal Spirit. They love and enjoy each other. As they interact together, it's like a Great Dance – they are always seeking to draw us in to the laughter, joy and creativity of their relationship. This is what makes Heaven, heavenly.

The total purity of God's character is revealed in the brilliant light of his holiness, the glowing warmth of selfless love, and his absolute truthfulness. He is the same. From eternity to eternity – he is God. Three-in-One, loving and honouring one another. He is always these things without effort or conflict. He is always being what he is being. Their full and rich life, constantly radiates joy so complete, so boundless that one touch of it would be enough to unmake us. The grandeur and magnificence of the Three-in-One tower above us like mountains taller than we can imagine – and still his voice calls us on into himself.

Consider the greatness of his descent. He became an ordinary man in a world filthy with selfishness, pride, greed and lust. He didn't just touch these things in passing – he sank into the pits of hell to plumb the deepest depravity of the worst of humanity. We'll never know what these words cost, *'God made him who had no sin to be sin for us.'* [7] He suffered more in hell than any person ever before or since. He was undefiled; yet he soaked up the defilement and absorbed the punishment of every man and woman. Wow! The greater his holiness, the greater we know his love is. He came down from the height of his holiness and joy into the darkest pit of our guilt. His love is greater – always greater.

WE SEEK A GOD BEYOND US

Mystery: the God who is never static though always at rest; always becoming yet also unchanging. The greater he is, the greater the mystery. He is always higher, wider, and deeper than we have yet discovered. Every day he is revealing to us more of the mystery of his being. The one who is 'being what he is being and becoming what he is becoming' has made us unique, so we can uncover some hidden pathway of his nature no one else could ever find.

This is the real quest. As God is eternally unfolding himself, he invites you into his heart on a vast journey of exploration. We will never get to the end of Him. There is always more. *'Great is the Lord and greatly to be praised,'* says the Psalmist *'His greatness is unsearchable'*.[8] That is our mind-blowing task: to search out the unsearchable greatness of God; to know the love of Christ which goes way beyond our knowing; to explore the richness of his Spirit which is limitless and inexhaustible.

Truly our God is amazing! It's just as well we have eternity. We're going to need it – and more!

We begin this search here and now – and the pull of his love draws us 'further in and higher up' as C. S. Lewis says.

Death becomes irrelevant, except that it removes from us the hindrance of a fallen world, and a rather rebellious body of flesh. It takes away the veil that hides heavenly things, and opens them to us for ever. But it also removes from us any further opportunity of bringing glory to Christ here on earth, by growing in him. Plus as we do, it widens the smile on his face!

Use your life wisely. It matters what you do because the quest that begins in faltering fashion here in this sin-grimed earth, goes on to find consummation in eternity. It's your God-given privilege and eternal joy; to go on and on into the heart of God. The way before you is planned for you alone – to know and reveal him as he was never revealed before. This is what the Bible means when it says that *'we impart a secret and hidden wisdom of God, which God decreed before the ages "for our glorification'*. [9] Uncovering layer upon layer of his glory, **we** will be transformed from one degree of glory to another.

WE SERVE A GOD WHO HAS PROMISED US THE KINGDOM

In the Lord's promises to the seven churches in Revelation 6, we see the unfolding of his destiny for us. These conditional promises are given to those who never give up fighting the temptations and pressures of the world, their fallen human nature and the Devil himself. To the extent that we allow God to reign in these areas – we will be overcomers **and** enter these blessings.

*'To him who overcomes I will give the right to eat from the
tree of life which is in the paradise of God.'*[10a]

This first promise reverses the effect of the Fall for those who
overcome, repenting and returning passionate love to God –
putting Him first. It gives them the right to eat from heaven's
tree of life, forever to be filled with the life of God.

*'He who overcomes will not be hurt at all by the
second death.'*[10b]

These people have lost everything for the sake of Christ;
suffering, poor and persecuted, they have nothing left to lose.
When all that is not of God is burned up, they will suffer no
pain. They are utterly alive. May we be so.

*'To him who overcomes I will give some of the hidden
manna. I will also give him a white stone with a new name
written on it known only to him who receives it.'*[10c]

Some live in places where there is much occult activity and
rampant immorality. If they are faithful, Jesus promises he
will mysteriously sustain and feed them with heavenly food.
He will also give them their new identity, an inner assurance
that, 'At last I know who I am. I belong.'

*'To him who overcomes and does my will to the end, I will
give authority over the nations – He will rule them with an
iron sceptre, He will dash them to pieces like pottery – just
as I have received authority from my Father. I will also give
him the morning star.'*[10d]

Corruption in the Church can only be overcome by total commitment to the will of God. To such people are promised two blessings: authority from Jesus like he received from his Father; and the power to shine out in the darkest moment – the hour before dawn.

> *'He who overcomes will like them be dressed in white. I will never blot out his name from the book of life, but will acknowledge his name before my Father and his angels.'*[10e]

Churches may have the appearance of life but still be dead. If we do his works: touch the hurting world with his compassion, refuse to compromise with immorality; he will clothe us in white to parade us before all heaven. Imagine being led out, honoured before all those angels – totally beats the Cup Final, an Olympic Gold, or even the Superbowl!

> *'Him who overcomes I will make a pillar in the temple of my God. Never again will he leave it. I will write on him the name of my God and the name of the city of my God the new Jerusalem which is coming down out of heaven from my God, and I will also write on him my own new name.'*[10f]

If we dare to witness for Jesus even when we are weak and afraid; he will make us an essential part of heaven, building us in like pillars. He will reveal through us the intimate nature of God, the eternal destiny of the Church, and the new revelation of Christ himself.

> *'To him who overcomes I will give the right to sit with me*
> *on my throne, just as I overcame and sat down with my*
> *Father on his throne.'*[09]

When a church is affluent and feels full of spiritual blessings, God often gets frozen out. But if we recognise our need, open up to him, let him share his life with us, and go with him through the cross, we shall overcome. He will lift us up to his throne to sit with him and reign with him.

This astonishing pattern of blessing starts with eternal life. It progresses through the pledge of new identity, into Christ-like authority over the nations, glorification before the angels, new revelation of Christ himself – and finally sits us on the throne of the Lord Jesus!

WE SHALL REIGN WITH HIM

Only God could have conceived such a daring plan – that we should share his throne and reign with him over the universe for ever and ever. Before you accuse me of delusional self-importance, just look at Revelation 22:4-5:

> *'They shall see his face, and his name shall be on their*
> *foreheads. And night shall be no more; they need no light of*
> *lamp or sun, for the Lord God will be their light, and **they***
> ***shall reign for ever and ever'**.*

Where do we go now?…
The answer is, 'Where no one has ever gone'.

As we see him, we shall be like him: because he reigns we shall share his sovereignty for ever. This does not lessen his glory – it increases it. He is glorified in his children. So here is the meaning of all the pain and hardship, all the cost and difficulty of the Christian life. *'I consider that our present sufferings are not worth comparing with the glory that will be revealed in us.'*[11]

Our pain in time is tied up with glory in eternity.

A new universe, a new earth with no evil, suffering or pain any more – this is what we are promised! As C. S. Lewis put it in *The Last Battle*: 'we then begin the real story, of which all that happened before was only the prologue and title page'. That is where it all starts.

God made you for himself. He made you because, having fathered you in eternity before the world was made, or the universe exploded into being from the Word – he loved you. He loves you still. He has called you into the centre of his loving, into his heart. No one else will do. You must go. Though you are completely superfluous; he has made you absolutely necessary; necessary to himself, to his angels, to the Church – and even to me.

So go, go on into his heart.

BOLDLY GO:
Knowing that the Maker awaits you in all the richness of his eternal fatherhood. Knowing that the Son waits to show you the marks of his love for you, so that your heart may exult with love for him. Knowing that the Spirit of God will be your

constant companion for ever, filling you with the wild freedom of his holy life. Knowing that the mystery of your being was something treasured in the Trinity from eternity, and now the secret is to be shared with you.

GO:

In the covenant-keeping Love of the Father, in the exuberant resurrection Life of the Son, and in the laughing, leaping Liberty of the Holy Spirit. Knowing that you have been called – to boldly go where no one has gone before.

God bless you.

EPILOGUE:
TO INFINITY
AND BEYOND

EPILOGUE... TO INFINITY AND BEYOND!

Death. It comes to all of us. But what's it like? Just for a moment, imagine passing through that dark doorway. Suddenly your eyes are filled with light that would be blinding, if it were earthly. But this is heavenly. As you look around, you are astonished by the splendour, and your first thought is, 'Am I in the right place?'

Immediately the answer comes, "You are".

You're aware of eyes more penetrating, tender and compassionate, than any you've ever seen. You know as he looks into you, he's seeing into the parts you've never allowed anyone, even yourself to see. You look down, instantly realising that the place is splendid, but you are not – yet. There are scars, some of them perfectly healed and in their way beautiful. But others are angry and infected. You hear a question, "Can I touch those – they need healing?"

Instinctively, you know this is going to hurt. Yet you want it more than you've ever wanted anything. The moment you say, "Yes", his touch on those hurts miraculously and meticulously brings to mind ancient wounds, bereavements, losses, sorrows – and they are lifted off you.

Now you are aware that part of your woundedness was anger, resentment, bitterness, guilt and even unforgiveness. You see it, unforgiveness is like drinking poison and waiting for the other guy to die.

Those eyes are lovingly scanning you.

"Time to let go of all that, I think."

"Yes, Lord." A gladder 'yes' than you've ever said. You feel the withdrawing of every deep-rooted tendril. You become aware: 'every last bit of things I hung on to for so many years is gone.'

When you look down, you are magnificent, as glorious as your surroundings.

His smile is like crinkly star-dust. "Nice to see you looking yourself at last."

It's been a huge process, drawn-out. But this is Heaven's time. Though it felt long to you, it was less than the blink of an eye. He smiles even more, "Happy now?" You realise you are. Happier than you ever dreamed was possible. So happy it feels almost indecent. Guilt has vanished. Every heartbreak and bereavement, every wound of confusion and fear has gone. Every pain has been beautifully reset into the context of his love. You see how everything – even what should not have been – has been made perfect. You look back and see only glory. Smile the biggest ever smile, ever. He smiles back. "Time to join the party, I think."

We will be remade – and it will be glorious.

NOTES

Chapter 1
1. 1 Corinthians 15:19 NRSV
2. Revelation 12:9-11JBP
3. Micah 6:8 GNB
4. Psalm 18:19; 37:23 ESV

Chapter 2
1. 2 Timothy 4:7-8 NRSV
2. See Luke 2:29-32 ED
3. Dr. A.T Bradford, The Jesus Discovery, Templehouse Publishing, 2010
4. Luke 2:49 GNB
5. Luke 4:18-19 NIV
6. Luke 4:43 NRSV
7. John 8:28-29 NRSV
8. John 5:19 NRSV
9. Mark 10:45 NLT
10. John 12:27; 13:1MSG
11. John 13:3 NIV
12. John 18:4 NIV
13. John 19:28 MSG
14. John 19:30 MSG

Chapter 3
1. Ecclesiastes 3:11 NLT
2. Judges 16:28 NLT
3. 1 Corinthians 3:12-15 NIV

Chapter 4
1. Winston Churchill, Mansion House, 10 November 1942
2. Genesis 1:26 NLT
3. Genesis 1:27 NLT
4. Genesis 2:24-25 ESV
5. Genesis 3:15 NLT
6. Luke 1:35 NLT
7. John 10:34-35 NIV

Chapter 5
1. Matthew 3:11; Mark 1:8; Luke 3:16; John1:33 NIV
2. Acts 1:5 NIV
3. I Corinthians 12:13 ESV
4. Acts 11:16 ESV
5. Acts 2:32-33 NLT
6. Luke 11:13 NKJV
7. 2 Corinthians 3:17 NIV

Chapter 6
1. Ephesians 1:4; Colossians 1:22 MSG
2. 1 Peter 2:9 GNB
3. Galatians 5:6 ESV
4. Mark 12:30-31 ESV
5. 1 John 4:19 ESV
6. Romans 12:1 NLT
7. Billy Bray, the King's Son, Epworth Press
8. 1 Corinthians 14:26 NSRV
9. 1 Corinthians 14:40 NKJV

Chapter 7
1. 2 Kings 7:9 GNB
2. Mark 8:35; 10:29 NLT
3. Mark 8:38; Luke 9:26 NIV
4. Matthew 28:19-20 NIV
5. Romans 10:9-10 NIV
6. 1 Timothy 1:1-4 NKJV
7. Galatians 5:1 MSG
8. 2 Timothy 1:7 NCV
9. Matthew 3:2 NIV
10. 2 Corinthians 4:6 NKJV
11. Psalm 136:1 NLT
12. Psalm 103:1 NIV
13. Galatians 5:24 NLT
14. Exodus 3:5-6 MSG
15. Deuteronomy 34:10 MSG
16. 2 Corinthians 4:6 NRSV/ESV

Chapter 8
1. Winston Churchill, History of the Second World War, Vol. 1. Writing of 10 May, 1940, when the King asked him to form a government.
2. See Aldous Huxley, Ends and Means, p. 270.
3. Steve Turner, A Way with Words, Razor Books, 1979.
4. John 5:39-40 NLT
5. Jeremiah 4:19 ESV/NRSV
6. 2 Timothy 2:15 Amp
7. Matthew 22:29 MSG

NOTES

Chapter 9

1. Revelation 12:7-9 NRSV/ESV
2. Exodus 17:1-7 NIV
3. Exodus 3:5 NLT
4. Ephesians 6:12 JBP
5. Ephesians 6:13 JBP
6. Ephesians 6:14-17 JBP
7. Ephesians 6:18 ESV
   (Compare Colossians 4:2 ESV)
8. Luke 4:9-11NIV
9. Matthew 25:14-30 NIV

Chapter 10

1. Winston Churchill, 18 June 1940
2. Luke 21:25-26; 28 NIV
3. Luke 21:24 NLT
4. Matthew 5:10-11 GNB

Chapter 11

1. Quoted in, Praying with The English
   Mystics, Triangle Books, 1990
2. Hebrews 2:9 MSG
3. Revelation 12:11 MSG
4. 1 Peter 4:17 MSG
5. Matthew 5:6 GNB
6. Psalm 90:2 ESV
7. 2 Corinthians 5:21 NIV
8. Psalm 145:3 ESV/RSV
9. 2 Corinthians 2:7 RSV
10. a. Revelation 2:7 NIV
    b. Revelation 2:11b NIV
    c. Revelation 2:17 NIV
    d. Revelation 2:26-28 NIV
    e. Revelation 3:5 NIV
    f. Revelation 3:12 NIV
    g. Revelation 3:21 NIV
11. Romans 8:18 NIV

KEY:

Amp	Amplified Version
ED	Eric Delve (paraphrase)
ESV	English Standard Version
JBP	J. B. Phillips
MSG	The Message
NCV	New Century Version
NIV	New International Version
NLT	New Living Translation
NKJV	New King James Version
NRSV	New Revised Standard Version